The Psychology of Religion

A SHORT INTRODUCTION

WITHDRAWN

LIVERPOOL JMU LIBRARY

3 1111 01091 1301

LIVERPOOL
JOHN MOORES UNIVERSITY
AVRIL ROBARTS LRC
TITHEBARN STREET
LIVERPOOL L2 2ER
TEL. 0151 231 4022

RELATED TITLES PUBLISHED BY ONEWORLD

Christianity and other Religions: Selected Readings, edited by John Hick and Brian
   Hebblethwaite, ISBN 1–85168–279–1
Concepts of God: Images of the Divine in Five Religious Traditions, Keith Ward,
   ISBN 1–85168–064–0
Ethics in the World Religions, edited by Joseph Runzo and Nancy M. Martin,
   ISBN 1–85168–247–3
The Fifth Dimension, John Hick, ISBN 1–85168–191–4
Global Philosophy of Religion: A Short Introduction, Joseph Runzo,
   ISBN 1–85168–235–X
God,Chance and Necessity, Keith Ward, ISBN 1–85168–116–7
God, Faith and the New Millennium, Keith Ward, ISBN 1–85168–155–8
God: A Guide for the Perplexed, Keith Ward, ISBN 1–85168–323–2
Interfaith Theology: A Reader, edited by Dan Cohn-Sherbok, ISBN 1–85168–276–7
Inter-religious Dialogue: A Short Introduction, Martin Forward, ISBN 1–85168–275–9
Love, Sex and Gender in the World Religions, edited by Joseph Runzo and Nancy M.
   Martin, ISBN 1–85168–223–6
The Meaning of Life in the World Religions, edited by Joseph Runzo and Nancy M.
   Martin, ISBN 1–85168–200–7
The Phenomenon of Religion: A Thematic Approach, Moojan Momen,
   ISBN 1–85168–161–2
Pluralism in the World Religions: A Short Introduction, Harold Coward,
   ISBN 1–85168–243–0
Religion: A Beginner's Guide, Martin Forward, ISBN 1–85168–258–9
Scripture in the World Religions: A Short Introduction, Harold Coward,
   ISBN 1–85168–244–9
Sin and Salvation in the World Religions, Harold Coward, ISBN 1–85168–319–4

The Psychology of Religion

A SHORT INTRODUCTION

Kate M. Loewenthal

ONEWORLD

OXFORD

THE PSYCHOLOGY OF RELIGION: A SHORT INTRODUCTION

Oneworld Publications
(Sales and Editorial)
185 Banbury Road
Oxford OX2 7AR
England
www.oneworld-publications.com

© Kate M. Loewenthal 2000
Reprinted 2004

All rights reserved
Copyright under Berne Convention
A CIP record for this title is available
from the British Library

ISBN 1-85168-212-0

Cover design by Design Deluxe
Typeset by Saxon Graphics, Derby, UK
Printed and bound in India by Thomson Press Ltd

CONTENTS

ACKNOWLEDGEMENTS

Many thanks to the following people for all kinds of help and support:

My family – my dear parents, children, sons and daughters-in-law and grandchildren, and other relatives, especially to my husband Tali Loewenthal.

Leaders of the Jewish community, especially the Lubavitcher Rebbe, Rav J. Dunner, Rabbi S. Lew, Lady Amelie Jakobovits.

All those from whom I have learnt and by whom I have been helped. To name a few: Esther Cadaner, Leah Namdar, Yitzchok Loewenthal, Chana-Soroh Danow, Moshe Loewenthal, Rivka Lent, Brocha Werner, Freida Loewenthal, Sholi Loewenthal, Mendy Loewenthal, Zalmy Loewenthal – my children, who helped and (almost) never complained, and their husbands, wives and children.

Professor Michael Eysenck, Dr Andy MacLeod, Dr Marco Cinnirella, Vivienne Goldblatt, Dr Susan Cook, Guy Lubitsh, Rosemary Westley, Jean Richards, Coreen Willis – and other colleagues and collaborators at Royal Holloway, London University.

Dr Christopher Alan Lewis of the University of Ulster who read the manuscript and made many helpful suggestions, and all the editorial staff at Oneworld.

Kerry Bak, Joyce Paley, Feigy Rabin, Shoshana Segelman, Evadne Stern – among the many friends who shared experiences and practical support.

AN OVERVIEW

I read about the following episode in a book by a British explorer in early twentieth-century Africa (Darley, 1972). It happened near the then Sudanese–Abyssinian border.

Two men lived close to each other. One had three strong adult sons, while the other, an old man, had one young grandson, age sixteen. All subsisted on a diet of game and honey, and their most important possessions were beehives and honey pots. The old man and his grandson caught the other family – four men – taking their honey pots. The four thieves shouted out that they would kill the old man and his grandson, and then 'All the honey pots will be ours'. The first young man rushed at the very old man. As he did so, the young grandson lunged at the attacker and pierced him through the heart with his spear, killing him. The second brother stumbled over the body, and the young boy pierced him through the neck, killing him. The third son lunged at the young boy, who side-stepped and gashed him down the side, without killing him. The wounded man and his father fled, and never bothered the old man and his grandson – or their bees – again. Major Darley recounted that he saw the young boy a few days later and congratulated him on his prowess. The boy replied 'How do you suppose it possible that a little boy like I am could kill two big men, and wound another, unaided? It was the act of God (*shauri ya Mungu*), for they were doing evil'.

Major Darley commented that he found that 'all people who live near nature believe in God'. Those who do not are 'too well-fed' and protected from danger by the amenities of civilized living.

Here is a similar observation, made by Rampal, an Indian immigrant to Britain in the 1960s:

'In India, there are many temples, mosques and churches. English people have no religion now. Few young people go to church, only the old men and women. Many English people even openly profess to have no belief in God, and take it very ill if you say to them, "Brother, it is good to pray". They say, 'What I believe is my own business; if I want to pray, then I will pray – if not, then I won't.' I suppose that English people have lost their religion because they lack no comforts. They are so well looked after by their government that they neither pray nor save; they take no thought for tomorrow. If the government were to declare that from next week no one would be allowed to draw National Assistance, then they would all surely run to church to pray to God for help.'

Quoted in Sharma, 1971

Both Major Darley and Rampal raise some issues that are fundamental to this book, but which psychologists have only recently begun to attend to. Their conclusion that material prosperity and the amenities of civilization breed Godlessness may have a grain of truth, but may be too simple. Nevertheless they raise the fundamental issues of why, when and how religious behaviours, ideas and feelings come about.

Students of history, sociology and anthropology are interested in people and groups of people, what they do and what they did – and why. It has always been recognized that religion is a powerful force in human society, associated with the strongest feelings and dramatic behaviour – sometimes admirable and sometimes horrible – and with powerful social forces. All serious students of the social sciences appreciate that they cannot reach any understanding of human society without knowledge of religion and religious institutions. But in the past, psychologists have generally stood apart from all others interested in religion and how it affects what people think and do.

This book looks first at the uneasy relationship that has existed between psychology and religion, and at how it has changed and developed. The psychology of religion is maturing as a field of study. Our understanding has progressed beyond the anti-religious polemics and pro-religious apologetics that were once often offered under the psychology of religion label.

The book then considers how the scientific psychological study of religious behaviour, thought and feeling has been affected by having been largely confined to the study of Western Christianity.

A detailed examination of religious behaviour includes a consideration of prayer, religious discourse, and other religious behaviour. We pay particular attention to religious conversion. Two chapters on the 'inner life' look at religious thoughts – beliefs, faith, experience – and religious feelings, including the emotional aspects of faith, and some of the negative emotions that might be associated with religion, such as guilt and shame. The second of these two chapters concludes by looking at the relations between religion and psychopathological states, particularly depression and schizophrenia.

Finally the book looks at some of the possible effects of religion on behaviour, thoughts and feelings. This includes an examination of the questions of how moral beliefs develop and affect behaviour, and, more controversially, how religion both makes and unmakes prejudice, and the relations between religion, identity and self-esteem.

1 PSYCHOLOGY AND RELIGION

WHAT IS PSYCHOLOGY?

What is psychology? I believe that it involves observing people, recording those observations and trying to interpret what has been observed and recorded.

The Hutchinson's Encyclopedia supports this belief. It says that *psychology is the 'systematic study of human ... behaviour'*, and that psychology includes the study of 'the roles of instinct ... culture ... and the functioning of thought, intelligence and language' (Hutchinson, 1994). My dictionary of psychology dwells on its task of definition for several pages, but it starts confidently enough. It says that psychology is the 'branch of science dealing with behaviour, acts or mental processes, and with the mind, self or person who behaves or acts or has the mental processes' (English and English, 1958).

How, then, can we define the psychology of religion? Argyle and Beit-Hallahmi begin their classic textbook (in 1958 it was called *Religious Behaviour*, by Argyle alone, in 1975, *The Social Psychology of Religion*, and in 1997 the title was *The Psychology of Religious Behaviour, Belief and Experience*, with Beit-Hallahmi as first author) with the terse promise that they will 'present the main empirical findings from social surveys, field studies and experiments about religious behaviour, beliefs and experience' (Argyle and Beit-Hallahmi, 1975)

All of this would allow me to maintain that psychology is the study of behaviour, thought and feeling, and that the *psychology of religion is the study of religious behaviour, thought and feeling*. But in the late 1990s, am I allowed to be so simplistic?

For example, two important 1990s textbooks on the psychology of religion did not define psychology (Batson, *et al*. 1993; Wulff, 1997). Perhaps this was because the intended readers were psychologists, and needed no definition. But both these and other contemporary works in the psychology of religion struggled with a more difficult problem. What is the psychology of religion? This was seen to be a little problematic because of the range of approaches in psychology. It was seen to be very problematic because of the difficulties in defining religion.

WHAT IS RELIGION?

Some scholars have suggested that defining religion is either impossible, or that it is such a major enterprise that we could not attempt it in a short book like this one. Wulff (1997) suggests that a 'satisfactory definition (of religion) has eluded scholars to this day', and that Smith (1963) has demonstrated that 'the noun religion ... (is) not only unnecessary but inadequate to any genuine understanding'. Brown (1987) spent many pages – over 100 – on the problems of defining, analysing and measuring religion and its many parameters. Capps (1997) has argued that the definitions of religion offered by eminent scholars reflect the personal biographies of those scholars.

This is a bit depressing because it suggests that there is no way to start this book! Defining religion is too difficult, so we cannot say what the psychology of religion is about, if we follow the subtle understandings of Wulff, or Brown, or Capps. We will have to be more grounded.

Down to earth, English and English (1958) suggested that religion is 'a system of attitudes, practices, rites, ceremonies and beliefs by means of which individuals or a community put themselves in relation to God or to a supernatural world, and often to each other, and ... derive a set of values by which to judge events in the natural world'.

Loewenthal (1995) suggested that the major religious traditions have a number of features of belief in common:

* there exists a non-material (i.e. spiritual) reality;
* the purpose of life is to increase harmony in the world by doing good and avoiding evil;
* (in monotheistic religions) the source of existence (i.e. God) is also the source of moral directives.

- In addition, all religions involve and depend on social organization for communicating these ideas.

Common features of religions thus included beliefs and behaviours about *spiritual reality, God, morality, purpose, and* finally the *communication* of these. Some would include atheism, agnosticism and 'alternative faiths' as religious postures involving a relationship with God (e.g. Rizzutto, 1974).

We are aware of differences between people with respect to religion. If I walk a few yards in the main street of the very polyglot area of North London in which I live, different styles of dress will proclaim many features of affiliation and piety. I see Muslim women, some with head covered, some with both head and face covered, and some with neither covered. I see Jewish women, some with a wig, some with a hat, some with both, and some with neither; Sikh men with and without turbans; Afro-Caribbeans who are identifiable (I think) as Christian (sober clothes), Rastafarian (dreadlocks), or neither. Jewish men wear fur or felt hats, white or black socks, surtouts, or other signs of affiliation to one of over a dozen different Hasidic sects which flourish locally. Sometimes I cannot translate the signs of identity and piety. But as a psychologist I do not have to rely on the language of clothes. I can ask questions.

In practice, the psychologist studying religion will often wish to assess religion, religiosity, or the extent to which a person engages in different kinds of religious behaviours and beliefs. One might start with a simple, single question about belief:

◆

A SINGLE-DIMENSIONAL MEASURE OF RELIGIOSITY

Mark the line to indicate how true the statement is for you. Place your mark over to the left if the statement is completely true, over to your right if completely untrue for you, or anywhere in between to indicate how true or untrue the statement is for you.

COMPLETELY TRUE	COMPLETELY UNTRUE

I believe in God ———————————————————————

◆

Is this too simple? Glock and Stark (1965) thought so. They suggested that social scientists might conceive of religious activity as involving five different 'dimensions', all of which might be independent of each other – at least in theory. For example a person who has a lot of mystical experiences may not necessarily engage in every prescribed religious ritual activity. Glock and Starks' dimensions are:

- *experiential* – the extent to which the person has religious experiences;
- *ritual* – the extent to which the person engages in religious ritual practices;
- *belief* – the extent to which the person subscribes to commonly or traditionally endorsed beliefs;
- *intellectual* – the extent of knowledge about religious teaching, tradition, etc.;
- *application* – a fifth dimension reflecting the extent to which the first four are applied in daily life.

This sort of 'dimensional' approach has been quite hard to operationalize; that is, to define in such a way that meaningful measurements can be made. Some psychologists of religion have queried whether it really matters which aspects of religious behaviour, experience, belief, etc. we measure, since all tend to co-vary one with the other. Wearing and Brown (1972), for example, reported a general 'religiosity' factor underlying a wide range of measures of religious activity and beliefs. Sometimes, of course, it *is* important to look at particular aspects of religious activity or belief. But if we want a general measure of religiosity, the following are popular and reliable (Loewenthal, 1995):

- *affiliation* – whether the person belongs to a religious group;
- *identity* or *self-definition* – whether the person defines themselves as religious (or Christian, Muslim, Jewish or whatever category the investigator is interested in);
- *belief in God.*

These are simple measures that will give us little more than a yes/no answer to a single question. If we want to sample a *range* of behaviours and beliefs there may be problems because of the specificity of behaviours and beliefs endorsed by different religious traditions and denominations. For example, the Francis Scale of Attitude Towards Christianity

(Francis, 1993b) is widely used as a measure of religiosity. It includes items such as:

- I know that Jesus helps me;
- I (do not) think the Bible is out of date.

These could be inappropriate questions to ask people from other religious traditions. In the same vein, Littlewood and Lipsedge (1981, 1998) needed quite different types of questions to discover the extent of 'religious interest' in people from different religious groups. Here are some examples of the questions they needed for Christians and for Jews, followed by some further questions developed recently for Muslims by Hanifa Khan (in preparation):

◆

RELIGIOUS INTEREST QUESTIONNAIRE

Examples of questions for Christians
Did the miracles in the Bible really happen?
Do you help with running your church?
Before making important decisions do you consult the Bible or pray?
To lead a good life is it necessary to have some religious belief?
Would you say you have ever had a personal religious experience?
Examples of questions for Jews
Do you attend the synagogue on the Day of Atonement?
Do you generally eat kosher food at home?
Do married women in your family generally wear a sheitel (wig)?

Littlewood and Lipsedge 1998

RELIGIOUS ACTIVITY QUESTIONNAIRE

Examples of questions for Muslims
Do you pray five times a day?
Do you observe the dress code?
Are you careful to eat according to religious rules?

Khan, in preparation

◆

To overcome this difficulty (of the specificity of rules in different religious traditions), and to enable comparisons to be made across different cultural-religious groups, Loewenthal and MacLeod developed a short measure, shown here.

◆

RELIGIOUS ACTIVITY QUESTIONNAIRE

How often do you attend (church, synagogue, mosque, place of worship)? (circle one)
DAILY/ WEEKLY/ MONTHLY/ OCCASIONALLY/ NEVER
How often do you study religious texts? (circle one)
DAILY/ WEEKLY/ MONTHLY/ OCCASIONALLY/ NEVER
How often do you pray? (circle one)
DAILY/ WEEKLY/ MONTHLY/ OCCASIONALLY/ NEVER

Loewenthal, MacLeod, *et al.*, 2000

◆

This measure has been quite useful, because it makes sense to people from different religious traditions. It is also reliable and valid; these two features are important for any psychological measure (Loewenthal, 1996; Jackson, 1996).

Having discussed some of the difficulties of definition and measurement, and having offered some solutions, it is tempting to finish this introduction. But let me just pass before you three cans of worms – not wide open, but just enough to glimpse inside.

A SHORT HISTORY OF THE UNEASY RELATIONSHIP BETWEEN PSYCHOLOGY AND RELIGION

The relationship between psychology and religion has been a very unhappy one for most of the twentieth century. Each domain has been seen as exclusive: if you are a psychologist you cannot take religion seriously, and if you are religious you cannot take psychology seriously. This has made for a climate in which the psychology of religion is seen as a paradox, an impossibility, or at best, an irreverent exercise which will undermine belief. Conversely, it has sometimes been seen as a ludicrous misapplication of science to something which is not worthy of scientific attention. I shall pick out two themes in tracing the origins of this unhappy and confrontational state.

The first theme is, simply, *Freud*. Freud's is probably the best-known name in the history of psychology, yet, paradoxically, hardly attended to in psychology courses in British universities. Freud was the inventor of the 'talking cure' – psychoanalysis – defined as a method of treating neurotic illnesses. His theories and clinical judgements shifted and developed in the course of his work. They were – and remain – controversial, and perennially fascinating. Freud was a keen and expert polemicist, and wrote a large number of very entertaining books intended for popular consumption, as well as many articles for medical and scientific readers. Several articles touched on religious issues, and four of his books (1927, 1928, 1930, 1939) were devoted entirely to the analysis of religion, often apparently to the great detriment of religion. For example *Totem and Taboo* traces the origins of religion and religious customs to a (historically) dubious single primal horde of people. The theory involved a bunch of males fighting over a bunch of females (plausible), which led to a taboo on incest (possible) and totemism, which was somehow collectively imprinted or transmitted to all later generations (muddled and much less plausible). Freud was good at telling a likely tale, and by the time he had finished with it, religion was written off as a bunch of primitive superstitions, neurotic rituals, and an illusion, which might have been comforting at one time, but which is no longer necessary in these enlightened times. Well-known outrageous statements by Freud include religion as a 'universal obsessional neurosis', which has succeeded because it spares the individual the labour of developing his or her own neurosis. Freud described God as a projection of the image of the father, and 'a system of wishful illusions together with a disavowal of reality, such as we find nowhere else but in amentia' (Freud, 1907, 1927). None of this endeared Freud to the orthodox religious establishment. Freud's other crime was to try and bring both sexuality and child abuse under psychiatric scrutiny. Child abuse was hastily withdrawn when the medical establishment of a century ago responded with an astonished, outraged and clearly disbelieving silence. Freud was conscious of being ostracized. However, sexuality stayed on the agenda and to this day, Freud's popular reputation rests on his supposed emphasis on sexuality. The following was quoted to me from a recent humorous newspaper article, and I offer it here because it epitomizes Freud's modern reputation:
Why did the chicken cross the road?
It depends who you ask.
Why did Freud say the chicken crossed the road?

Freud said that the reason you are interested in why the chicken crossed the road is because of your hidden sexual conflicts.

Describing some Christian attitudes to psychotherapy, Esau (1998) suggested that evangelical Christians may feel that the 'psychological perspective of Freud ... was outside the realm of faith. It was viewed, alongside Darwinism, as the enemy of faith and the believer'. 'Spiritual counsel was the means (of help) ... that was where deliverance would come ... evangelicals believed they were defending their faith by considering that the emotionally disturbed had sinned in some way ... the faithful had to remain faithful; the enemy was clear.'

In a nutshell, then:

- *Freud equals psychology.* Although psychologists scantily teach his theories, and many psychologists are doubtful about the scientific value of his theories and the clinical efficacy of his methods, he is still the best-known psychologist.
- *Freud is disreputable.* He wrote a lot about the importance for psychiatry, medicine and science of understanding sexual urges, therefore he was interested in sex.
- *Freud is anti-religious.* He actually said some very perceptive and positive things about religion, and Bettelheim (1983) has even argued that Freud's entire psychoanalytic oeuvre was a spiritual venture. But Freud said too many naughty, though witty and plausible, things about religion to suit many of the devout, and fairly enough, the general thrust of his writing was not seen as sympathetic to religion.

We could say that Freud was the single most important force in creating a gulf between psychology and religion, and in causing any ventures in the psychology of religion to be seen as irreverent and destructive to religion.

However, we could also say that Freud was expressing and responding to a *Zeitgeist*. In the intellectual climate of the first half of the twentieth century, science was seen as concerned with the observable, and religion with the unobservable.

Therefore the second theme in the history of the relationship between psychology and religion is the view that *scientific psychology and religion cannot be reconciled*. There are several angles on this. The simplest is that empirically, religion was described ('scientifically') as a disappearing phenomenon, therefore not worth studying. It was (and to some extent still is) seldom written about in psychology books (see Figure 1.1). Religious behaviour and religious influences on behaviour are not seen as worthy objects of scientific attention. Most psychology textbooks simply do not index religion. Psychiatry and religion have a parallel history of discord (Foskett, 1996).

In my undergraduate psychology degree, I can only recall one brief discussion of religion. I did my degree a very long time ago, in the early 1960s. At that time, Skinnerian psychology was considered quite important. I remember we had a lot of lectures about it. In the opening lecture, the lecturer explained carefully that a hungry rat could be placed in an apparatus called a 'Skinner box' (named after its inventor, B.F. Skinner). This box was a bleak and callous environment, with blank metal walls, relieved by (normally) just one lever, and one food box. A really exciting Skinner box might have two bars, or even deliver painful electric shocks through the floor, but normally one bar and one food box was the limit of entertainment. When the rat pressed the bar, a food pellet appeared. The lecturer explained that when the 'operant behaviour' (bar-pressing) was reinforced (with food) regularly and frequently (continuous reinforcement), the rat would bar-press rather slowly. If however reinforcement were random and *in*frequent, the rat would bar-press rapidly, eagerly, even frenziedly. My recollection is of the lecturer turning to the audience and smiling triumphantly. He said he thought that enthusiastic religious behaviour could be explained in terms of the reinforcement contingencies he had just described. In religion, rewards were random and infrequent, leading to eager or frenzied behaviour. I do not recall any other discussion of religion or religious behaviour in my undergraduate psychology course.

In recent years, as we shall see, psychologists have taken a much more sophisticated interest in religious behaviour, thought and feeling. Spilka *et al.* (1981) studied references to religion in introductory psychology textbooks in the 1950s compared to the 1970s. The mean number of citations of work about religion per volume was small – 4.6 in the 1950s, and even lower (2.6) in the 1970s. They detected two significant changes in the quality of treatment of religion between the 1950s and 1970s. There was a significant rise in the amount of neutral, objective treatment of religion, and a significant fall in negative explanations. There was also a small rise in the amount of actual research reported.

There are other signals of growing reconciliation between psychology and religion:

• A number of comments about psychology's (and psychiatry's) past neglect of religion have appeared, and concern that this neglect should be rectified (Neeleman and Persaud, 1996; Paloutzian, quoted in Hester, 1998).

• The number of references to religion and religious issues and influences is growing in psychology textbooks. Although Spilka *et al.* detected a drop between the 1950s and the 1970s, described above, there has been a rise since then. Thus my perusal of the indexing of religion in ten undergraduate textbooks on social psychology and on personality – two areas of psychology in which one would expect religion to be attended to – suggested an interesting change in the first half of the 1990s (Figure 1.1).

• The number of publications on psychology and religion is growing. Figure 1.2 suggests a surge in the first half of the 1990s, similar to the surge suggested in Figure 1.1.

Figure 1.1   Mean number of references to religion per book, in undergraduate textbooks on social pyschology and personality

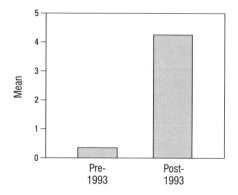

Figure 1.2   Average annual number of publications in religion and mental health, 1991–1996 (based on Dein and Loewenthal, 1998)

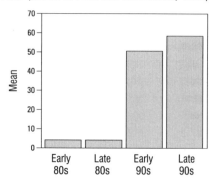

- There has been a number of recent attempts to integrate aspects of religion and psychology. One ambitious attempt is Watts and Williams (1988) *The Psychology of Religious Knowing*, in which the authors explore the relationship between contemporary cognitive psychology and religious knowing. Another is Spero's (1992) careful argument that one may need to accept God's existence to explain the facts of people's relationships with God. Grace and Poelstra (1995) produced a special edition of the *Journal of Psychology and Theology* exploring the integration of psychology and theology in undergraduate psychology courses.
- The psychology of religion can be seen as a genuine social scientific activity, and courses in this area are undertaken by students of any or no religious background. To quote an exchange between Paloutzian and Hester (Hester, 1998):

> (Hester) 'Does one have to have religious beliefs to study the psychology of religion?'
> (Paloutzian) 'Whether or not one holds personal religious beliefs, one can study the psychology religion. Doing research in the psychology of religion does not require holding religious beliefs yourself. The leading scholars in the area include those who are religiously neutral, Catholics, Protestants, Jews, Mormons, atheists, and unknowns. You no more have to be religious to study psychology of religion than you have to be depressed in order to study depression, or to be prejudiced in order to study racial attitudes'.

In essence, the initially poor relationship between psychology and religion has made it difficult for the psychology of religion to develop. However, an improvement in the relationship has caused – and is signalled by – a growing quantity and improved quantity of work on the psychological aspects of religion, and on the impact of religion.

SPIRITUALITY AND RELATED ISSUES

Eventually, after a troubled start, the psychology of religion began to develop and flourish during the 1970s and 1980s. But as one trouble receded, another loomed, or is beginning to loom. The new set of difficulties concerns the issue of spirituality, and the view that it is something different or separable from religion (Zinnbauer *et al.* 1997).

Signs include Wulff's (1997) argument that spirituality is possibly a contemporary alternative to religion in today's pluralistic society.

Spirituality might be what all religious-cultural traditions have in common. But it may also be a divisive issue.

Helminiak (1996) argued that the study of spirituality can be undertaken scientifically, and is 'different from the psychology of religion as generally conceived'. Zinnbauer *et al.* found a number of features that distinguished adults who defined themselves as religious (and also spiritual), from adults who defined themselves as spiritual but not religious. The most noteworthy differences were that those who said they were spiritual but not religious were more likely to engage in New Age religious beliefs and practices, but were less likely to be engaged with the beliefs and practices of traditional religions.

These suggestions are indicative of the growing feeling that spirituality is possible outside the context of organized or traditional religion.

GENDER

Public life and published life are predominantly masculine. This applies to the religious domain as well as to other areas. Saints and prophetesses and nuns can be female, but in the public arenas of religion, and in leadership roles, women are a minority. My desk is covered with books and journals and articles on the psychology of religion: over 80 per cent of the authors are men. Social-scientifically, the consensus seems to be that women's experiences may differ from the (masculine) 'norm'. Women's experiences of religion are private-domain, and they are harder to access.

In psychological studies, participants are often women, but the possibility of gender differences is often ignored. Where they have been attended to, gender differences are often described in ways that are pejorative to women. Notorious examples include Freud's suggestion that women's moral and religious development is weaker and more tenuous than that of men, and Kohlberg's (1969) claim that women's moral development is often less advanced than that of men. Gilligan (1993) made the vigorous claim that women's moral values were founded differently to those of men – men live in a world of individualistic assertion, women live in a world of caring. With good reason, Reich (1997) has asked if we need a theory for the religious development of women.

These are flickers of concern in an area of investigation in which the differences in quality between the social worlds and the experiences of women and men, girls and boys have often been overlooked.

SUMMARY

Psychology of religion was defined as the study of religious behaviour, thought and feeling, but some difficulties of definition were noted. Difficulties in defining and measuring religion were also noted, and some examples of general measures of religiosity were given. Finally, three problematic areas for the psychology of religion were described: the so-called conflict between scientific psychology and religion, the new claim that spirituality and religion are distinct issues, and the lack of attention given to possible differences between the religious experiences and behaviours of men and women.

2 RELIGION AND PSYCHOLOGY

THE INFLUENCE OF WESTERN CHRISTIANITY

Is the psychology of religion the psychology of Western Christianity? This question first came into my mind some years ago, when I first began reading on the psychology of religion. Based on his theories of personality and conditionability, H.J. Eysenck had suggested that religious attitudes and beliefs would be associated with introversion and neuroticism (Eysenck and Eysenck, 1985). Introversion involves low sociability and impulsivity, and neuroticism involves anxiety, depression, low self-esteem and tension (Eysenck, 1998). H.J. Eysenck thought that neurotic introverts would be conditioned more easily than other people, and thus be more susceptible to injunctions of all kinds, including religious injunctions. Numerous tests of H.J. Eysenck's suggestions were made, including those of Siegman (1963), who reported in the *British Journal of Social and Clinical Psychology*, that among Protestant students religiosity was associated with extraversion, while among Jewish students religiosity was associated with introversion.

For me this was a nice clear example of how relations between 'religion' and 'personality' could be quite different in different cultural–religious groups. In this case, Siegman reported exactly *reversed* relations between religion and introversion–extraversion among Protestants and among Jews.

As a postscript to Siegman's study, I should quote M.W. Eysenck's (1998) conclusion that when sex differences are partialled out, 'there is practically no convincing evidence that either extraversion or neuroticism is related to religiosity'.

But the moral of Siegman's early study may point to an enduring underlying difficulty in studying the psychology of religion. The difficulty is that the meanings of behaviours vary in different cultural–religious settings. Thus the interpretation and understanding of religion may be difficult for those with a 'Western' cultural framework, and, on a more subtle level, for those using the concepts and methods of 'Western' (Christian) psychology of religion (see box).

◆

THE MEANING OF BEHAVIOUR IN DIFFERENT CULTURAL–RELIGIOUS SETTINGS

Loewenthal (1995) describes the following misunderstanding between orthodox Jews and mental health professionals. Mr and Mrs B had a son who was having some difficulties in school. He was not keeping up with the class, was very restless and disruptive, and was being difficult at home. The school suggested they should take their son to see a psychologist. Mr and Mrs B were very indignant at this suggestion because someone else that they knew had done this, and had met with a total misunderstanding of the behavioural norms and values of the community. Mr and Mrs B had heard that a psychologist had come to watch this other boy and saw him swaying backwards and forwards over his book. This is normative behaviour in strictly-orthodox Jewish boys' schools. It is encouraged particularly when boys are praying and studying religious texts. The psychologist was reported to have said that she thought the boy was disturbed because of the way he was swaying. When the parents of the swaying boy pointed out that all the boys do it, the psychologist was alleged to have said, 'Perhaps they are *all* disturbed'.

Firth (1997) describes the importance to Hindus of the good death, one for which adequate preparation has been made, and which takes place at a good time and in a good place. It is better to die on the ground than on a bed, and Firth describes the tragic contretemps that can happen in British hospitals when a dying Hindu manages to get out of bed in order to die. Harassed nurses rush to replace the patient in the correct place (bed), while the dying victim becomes deeply depressed or agitated that the efforts they are making to die properly are being thwarted by the uncomprehending medical staff.

An early twentieth-century view of a black woman's religious activity resulted in the following horrifying misinterpretation. Evarts (1914) described a young Afro-American woman working in domestic service. She developed a stomach disorder and could not afford an orthodox medical practitioner, so she went to a West Indian herbalist. The herbal treatment was unsuccessful, and the herbalist was reported to have made unwelcome sexual advances. The young woman's behaviour became disturbed and she was sent to her sister's home, but did not calm down: '... She now became very sure that the herb doctor had put a spell on her and she read her Bible constantly to exorcise it. She was admitted to the Washington Asylum Hospital. While there she persisted in her refusal to eat or talk. She now thought the food was unholy and the people about her unholy. She read her Bible, and prayed all day long ...' Evarts continues with further details of this 'patient's' religious activities, with the strong implication that these were all indicative of 'dementia precox' (a diagnostic category roughly corresponding to schizophrenia). Even more chilling, is Evarts' comment that the case 'shows very well the primitive (sic) character of these people'.

◆

Are different religious traditions so different from each other that there can be no common ground in the ways in which psychologists understand them?

RELIGIONS AND THEIR ACCOUNTS OF BEHAVIOUR, THOUGHTS AND FEELINGS

In the remainder of this chapter different religious traditions will be considered with respect to:

- the kinds of qualities and behaviours that might be valued, and considered healthy and normative;
- how these qualities and behaviours might be misjudged by outsiders;
- how this might affect psychological understanding of religion in that particular religious tradition.

Of course it is difficult to consider themes in major religious traditions without stereotyping, over-simplifying, and ignoring important variations and minority views within religious traditions. These dangers have to be risked in the hope of offering some useful generalizations.

Finally, we will consider whether there are any common themes in the different religious traditions, and if so, what they might be. Commonalities between different religious groups might make it possible to test conclusions and ask similar questions across different groups.

Buddhism

Buddhism is one of the two major religious traditions of the East, with an estimated 150–200 million adherents worldwide. Although images of saints and statues of Buddha are revered by Buddhists, this is not a poly-theistic religion. In fact there is some scholarly debate whether Buddhism is theistic at all. Buddhism began about 1500 years ago in India, as a reaction against the instrumental, formalized, caste-dominated polytheism dominant at that time.

The two main forms of Buddhism are Theravada, which is regarded as a more classical and orthodox form of Buddhism, and Mahayana. Zen (meditative) Buddhism is a variety of Mahayana first practised in China and then developed in Japan. This form of Buddhism is perhaps the most widely known to many Westerners since it has been popularized in many English-language writings. The priestly life is esteemed in Buddhism, and this involves asceticism, discipline, and spending very large amounts of time on prayer and meditation. Most forms of Buddhism prescribe specific rituals and practices.

The fundamental teaching of Buddhism involves viewing an attachment to the world and its pleasures as the cause of pain. Self-mortification is also an extreme to be avoided. The founder of Buddhism, Gautama Buddha taught the 'middle path'. Life is fundamentally a process of suffering. As in Hinduism, transmigration and rebirth are not seen as progressive, and the central aim of religious belief and practice is to be liberated from attachment to the material. It is desire for the material that causes suffering. The eight-fold ('middle') path to freedom from suffering includes right thought, speech, action and mental attitudes. These lead to the cessation of pain, and to enlightenment, and nirvana, wherein the soul will not be reborn to further suffering.

Buddhist psychology is quite popular in the West (Valentine, 1989; de Silva 1996). In fact I passed a London bus yesterday advertising a perfume called Zen: the slogan suggested that if I bought it, I would be 'calm amid the chaos'. It has been suggested that religious practices and thoughts will enhance psychological well-being. Manne-Lewis (1986) describes the cognitive changes involved in enlightenment, which entails a profound cognitive restructuring and ultimately a state in which 'all personal constructs have been eradicated'.

De Silva (1996) describes two forms of Buddhist meditation. First, *samatha* (tranquillity), which involves progressive distancing from both external and internal stimuli, and second, *vispassana* (insight), which involves concentration exercises focusing on specific objects, and maintaining an undistracted mindfulness by which one becomes aware of all phenomena, and the impermanence of all things.

De Silva (1996), Shapiro (1982) and others have described various features of Buddhist psychology which are of interest to psychologists, and of possible therapeutic benefit. These include features of meditation, and methods of behaviour change such as using rewards to promote desirable behaviour.

Scotton (1998) has pointed out that Buddhist patients 'seek to understand the meaning of (their) problem(s), and what failed in his or her consciousness that led to that difficulty'. Buddhist patients may place more emphasis on psychological–interpersonal–spiritual context in understanding psychological difficulties. Scotton also mentions that Buddhist patients with psychological problems may present what seems like a pathological passivity – in the eyes of the Western observer.

One might wonder whether the emphasis on achieving a state of enlightenment in which attachment to materiality is eliminated, and in which personal judgements are not valued, might lead to states which could be seen as indifferent and too unreactive – to observers from other cultures and religious traditions. Are the concepts and measures appropriate to Western psychology of religion appropriate to Buddhism? For example, would the following have similar meanings and values to Buddhists, as to the Christians for whom the items were devised:

- 'I try hard to carry my religion over into all my other dealings in life.' This item assesses intrinsic religiosity (chapter 6). It is from the Allport-Ross (1967) religious orientation scale. To what extent does Buddhism offer a way of relating to 'other' dealings in life, other than detachment?
- 'What religion offers me most is comfort when sorrow and misfortune strike.' This is an extrinsic religiosity item from Allport and Ross. Here we might ask whether 'comfort' is a category alien to Buddhism? Further, a Buddhist might comment that 'sorrow' and 'misfortune' are only the result of faulty perception.

Christianity

Christianity provided the context for the development of the psychology of religion, and has by far the most adherents of the major religious traditions, with about 1,000 million people identified as Christians, mostly in Europe, the Americas and Australasia. Thus, Christianity dominates the economically dominant, 'developed' countries.

The major divisions of Christianity are into the Eastern and Western churches, and within the latter, into the Roman Catholic and the Protestant churches. The Protestant churches have fewer explicit regulations and doctrines than Roman Catholicism and Eastern Christianity. Protestantism is said to place greater emphasis on individual responsibility.

The fundamental belief is in the unity of God. The doctrine of the trinity (Father, Son and Holy Spirit) is also central, as is the idea that the death of Jesus atoned for the sins of humanity. Jesus is seen as especially chosen by God. Roman Catholics, and many other Christians, also accept the 'Ten Commandments', involving belief in one God and prohibiting idol worship, murder, theft, envy and sexual immorality. The Ten Commandments are a noteworthy legacy from the Judaic origins of Christianity. Other Jewish (Old Testament) writings are also valued in Christianity.

Catholics are religiously obliged to fast on prescribed days, attend mass and abstain from unnecessary work on Sundays and holy days, confess sins regularly, contribute to the support of the Church and observe marriage laws. In Britain and the USA, several varieties of Protestantism have overtaken Catholicism in terms of numbers of adherents, and in terms of political influence. The fundamentals of Christianity, as just described, are not disputed in Protestantism. The main differences between Catholicism and Protestantism are that specific religiousobligations are less firmly insisted upon in Protestantism. There is less investment of authority in the Church hierarchy, and greater emphasis on individual conscience. Between Protestant denominations, there are differences in doctrines, for example about the origins of sin, and how it is forgiven, and in emphasis upon love and joy.

There are a number of Christian groups distinguished by high degrees of active participation in group worship, including behaviours such as glossolalia ('speaking in tongues'), displays of grief at sinfulness, joy at being saved, and singing and dancing. Such evangelical/charismatic groups have a high proportion of Afro-Caribbean membership. One example of such a group is the African Methodist Episcopal Zion Church, which broke away from mainstream Methodism in the late eighteenth century as a result of race prejudice experienced by black church members. This charismatic style of Christianity is becoming increasingly popular among white people, and religious joy is a valued emotion in many hristian circles. A number of new charismatic-style Christian religious groups have emerged in recent years, and it can be argued that Christianity has a historical tradition of giving rise to such groups (Bainbridge, 1997).

Another important psychological aspect of Christianity relates to dogmas regarding sin. Sin is seen as the result of the misuse of human freedom. Human wilfulness is to have and to enjoy, to turn to self and to the things of this world and away from God. Suffering is the result of sin. Salvation involves justification, the removal of sin and its effects by one or more of penance, indulgence, confession, absolution and forgiveness. (Dodge, Armitage and Kasch, 1964; Solomon, 1965; Eliade, 1985). Although suffering is not seen as a desirable end in itself, it is seen as a gateway to renewal and rebirth. Guilt and forgiveness are thus important processes in Christian psychology.

Another strong tradition in Christianity of considerable psychological interest is mysticism, described evocatively by a pioneer in the psychology of religion, Rudolf Otto (1917), as the awesome experience of the numinous. Mystical experience is the topic of many tracts and poetic works by Christian saints and mystics (Wulff, 1997). Awe and religious ecstasy are valued states in the Christian mystical tradition.

Some pioneers of modern psychiatry and humane psychiatric treatment were strongly Christian-influenced, for example Tuke, a Quaker. The psychology of religion itself evolved in the context of Christian (generally Protestant) culture. Notable and influential figures in the psychology of religion who were heavily influenced by their Christian background included William James (1902), Rudolf Otto (1917), Paul Tournier (see Cox, 1998), Gordon Allport (1950) and C.G. Jung (1958). Mormons (Latter-day Saints) have taken a keen interest in the development of the psychology of religion. Barlow and Bergin (1998) have suggested that some psychopathologies may be fostered by the Mormon lifestyle and beliefs, such as being a member of a minority group, mistrusting orthodox medicine, authoritarianism, and superstitious spiritualism. Defection may also lead to adjustment problems. However, alternatively, they suggest that Mormon beliefs and lifestyle may promote psychological health. Many of these observations might apply to other Christian groups.

Hinduism

Hinduism is the religion of India, and in its broadest sense much of India's 500 million plus population may be said to be Hindu. There are also Hindus scattered around the Far East and many other countries where Indians have settled.

Hinduism developed from earlier religions of the Indian subcontinent, and there are many varieties. Hinduism is a pluralistic religion, tolerating a wide range of beliefs and practices. Its chief characteristics are its polytheism, overlying a fundamental monotheism wherein the lesser divinities are subsidiary aspects of one God. This infinite principle (God) is truly the sole reality and the ultimate cause and goal. There is a rigid religiously sanctioned caste system, now said to be becoming more flexible.

Religious worship (*puja*) is carried out in a shrine in the home, usually by women. Regular prayer, fasting, good thoughts and deeds, pilgrimage and reverence for elders are all aspects of the religious duties of the pious Hindu (Juthani, 1998). Transmigration of souls and reincarnation are important aspects of Hindu belief. The ultimate goal is infinity (God), and the attainment of this goal is prevented by *karma* (rebirth); following death and a sojourn in heaven or hell, the soul is reborn into a physical form determined by actions in the previous incarnation. This process of rebirth (*samsara*) is seen as potentially endless, and not progressive in any way. Misfortunes are seen as an aspect of *karma*. *Karma* may be escaped by *marga* – emancipation. There are different types of *marga* suited to various types of individuals. The principal types of *marga* are duty, knowledge and devotion.

Possibly the most striking features of Hinduism of interest to the psychologist are:

- *attitudes to misfortune*, which could appear stoical, patient and resigned to observers from other cultures;
- *treatment of mental illness*. In rural communities, where most (80 per cent) of India's population live, tolerance for bizarre behaviour is very high. A mentally-ill person will be taken to a healer within the community, and Hindu tradition and texts offer a wide range of possible therapeutic interventions (Bhugra, 1996). If such treatment is not successful, it is regarded as the family's duty to bear with the person. Craissati (1990) observed that use of Western psychiatry is rare. Campion and Bhugra (1998) describe some of the belief systems and practices used by healers in India. Mental illnesses may result from life stress, or the 'evil eye' (envy, ill-will from others), spirit possession, or the consequences of a previous life. Treatments include prayer, herbal- and aromatherapy, and music.

Islam

There are about 350 million Muslims, most of them Sunni. Another important group within Islam is the Shi'ite, with a third, smaller, mainly North African group, the Khawarij. Islam originated in the Middle East, where it is still the prevalent religion, but there are substantial numbers of Muslims in the Indian subcontinent and in some Far-Eastern countries, and there are said to be growing Islamic minorities in many developed countries. In Britain it is numerically the largest non-Christian religion (Clarke, 1988).

Islam is a monotheistic religion, and therefore by definition belief in God is a central tenet. In Arabic, Islam means submission to the will of God. There is a clear core of religious duties (the five pillars of Islam; Husain, 1998), which are relatively straightforward to specify. These include belief in God and the prophets, prayer, giving away a proportion of one's goods, fasting in the month of Ramadan, and pilgrimage. Modern Islam is said to originate with the prophet Mohammed, who is seen as a continuation of a line of prophets beginning with Adam, the first man.

The central feature of the Islamic view of sin is that sin involves forgetfulness of divine unity. The root of sin is pride and self-sufficiency. Reason is seen as playing an important role in the choice of right.

Islam has a long tradition of interest in mental health. The earliest recorded psychiatric institutions – established over a thousand years ago – were in Muslim countries. The mentally ill are viewed as 'the afflicted of Allah'. In the last decade a number of publications on the psychological aspects of Islam have appeared (El Azayem and Hedayat-Diba, 1994; Geels, 1996; Kose, 1996a, 1966b; Hedayat-Diba, 1997). One feature of some of these writings has been the emphasis on the psychological benefits of Islamic practice: 'Islam(ic) ... teachings have reference to care for the family, divorce and polygamy, concern for the welfare of parents and the aged, and concern for learning and work. Proscriptions against suicide, sexual perversions, crime and racial discrimination ... Muslims can enjoy healthy and balanced lives by following these teachings' (El Azayem and Hedayat-Diba, 1997). Muslims report that regular prayer (*salat*) is experienced as beneficial psychologically (Cinnirella and Loewenthal, 1999), and may prefer to try prayer and other religious means to alleviate psychological distress (Husain, 1998)

Esmail (1996) has argued that Islam offers 'a vision of community, self and self-realization which differ ... from the dominant philosophy of the modern West'. Esmail emphasizes the relative importance of community and communal ties in Islamic life.

Judaism

Numerically the smallest of the major religions, Judaism has had important influences on the development of the numerically and politically powerful traditions of Christianity and Islam. Worldwide there are 10–12 million Jews, mostly living in Israel, the USA and the former USSR, with smaller communities in many other countries.

Judaism is the oldest of the monotheistic religions. By definition, a central tenet is the belief in the unity of God. Jewish people are seen as the bearers of this belief. The Jewish people are obligated to practise a large number of different religious commandments, governing more or less the total life-style. Diet, sexual behaviour, work, business ethics and worship are among the areas to which religious law applies. Different Jewish groups may vary in degree of observance and in specific customs. A Jew is defined as one born from a Jewish mother, or who has converted according to Jewish law. Judaism is unusual among religions in that proselytization is generally not encouraged. Proselytization is not seen to be necessary for human betterment. Non-Jews are said to be righteous and to merit heavenly after-life if they believe in the unity of God and do not worship idols, are just, sexually moral, avoid cruelty and theft.

In recent years, world Jewry has come into conflict with the former Communist and Arab nations, and is beset with problems of secularization. However, there are signs of religious fervour in some sections, and of widespread strong attachment to Jewish tradition and history.

Religious scholarship is valued in Jewish tradition. There is a wide range of Jewish texts, ranging from the Pentateuch, through the Talmud and other legal texts, to the Kabbalistic and mystical literature. Most contain discussions of psychological and psychiatric interest.

Misfortune is seen as a warning to the individual to improve, and as a divine test of the individual; also as part of an overall divine plan in which everything is for the ultimate good. Misfortune is seen in Jewish mystical thought as part of a process involving reincarnation in which errors in previous incarnations are repaired – this repair process will achieve Messianic completion.

Features of contemporary Judaism that might have psychological impact include the beleaguered state of modern Israel, combined with the history of dispersion and persecution. Also important is the detailed nature of practical religious law (whether accepted or rejected by any given individual), the value placed on scholarship, and the importance of marriage and the family for religious life (Levitz, 1992; Loewenthal, 1995; Cooper, 1996).

It is also important to note that Jews are heavily represented in the psychiatric and psychological professions, and much writing in the psychology of religion is by Jews. The psychology of religion may often be at least as much about Judaism as it is about Christianity. The classic works of Freud (1907, 1927, 1930), Erikson (1958), Maslow (1964) and Fromm (1950) are well-known examples.

Other religions

There are many other traditional religions that have either fewer adherents or lesser impact on the world outside the community of adherents. They will not be considered here.

Other forms of religion include *religious syncretism*, in which beliefs and practices from different religious traditions in contact are blended. Syncretic religions have been described in parts of South America and the Caribbean, where some Christian practices have been combined with those of African (or other) religions, as in Cuban *Santeria*. Perez Y Mena (1998) suggests that the European-Christian influence on such religions has been exaggerated.

Finally, we should mention *new religious movements (NRMs)*, ('cults') in which there has been rapid growth since 1960. Typically these have charismatic leaders, who require total devotion from followers, and that they give up their connections with family and friends, and many habits such as smoking, alcohol, promiscuity. Many of these movements involve communal living, and earnings are given over to the movement. There is often strong emphasis on meditation, mysticism and spiritual 'highs'. (Paloutzian, 1983; Galanter, 1989). Examples include the Divine Light Mission, the Universal Church of the Reverend Sun Yung Moon ('Moonies'), Rashneesh, and forms of Wicca (which claims to be a development of traditional witchcraft). The latter is one of several so-called manifestations of 'New Age spirituality', and attracting current interest are a number of millennial groups. Some New Religious Movements are based on the Far Eastern religions, and many are surrounded by strong controversies. Bainbridge (1997) offers excellent descriptions and discussions of several recent and contemporary religious movements (see box).

Robert and Mary Ann originally trained as psychotherapists-clergy. They went on to attract friends into a form of psychological-spiritual therapy called Compulsions Analysis. Gradually the group formed close ties with each other, breaking away from the extended social network, and forming a tightly-knit group 'free from the social control that enforces conformity to the norms of the larger society'. Their new beliefs and practices centred around the central idea that people would 'naturally have the powers and wisdom of gods if these had not been stolen from them' perhaps in the intermissions between past lives. The right spiritual technology – psychological therapeutic exercises – can restore the person. The group renamed itself The Process, and Robert wrote a book describing how humanity is doomed, but 'we must be free', 'we shall be of the New Beginning'. The group relocated in the Bahamas, then returned to London to rescue under-age members who had been kidnapped by their indignant families. The group developed during the 1960s, flourished during the 1970s, and eventually fizzled out.

Bainbridge, 1997

A number of suggestions have been made about the psychological implications of belonging to a new religious movement. Some claim that members are weaned off destructive habits (such as drugs and sexual promiscuity), and that there is no evidence that the members are psychologically unbalanced before or after (see e.g. Richardson, 1985). Opponents accuse NRMs of brainwashing their members, and exploiting them, sexually, financially and otherwise. In recent years, several NRMs have been responsible for killings – either mass suicide as in Jonesville, or 'terrorism' as when the AUM movement killed a number of members of the public in the Tokyo subway system. NRMs have distinct social-psychological characteristics. The most important are probably the salience of group identity, and the speed and totality with which fundamental social, cognitive and life-style changes are demanded. Barker (1996) has discussed the mental health implications of these and other features of NRMs.

Common themes

We preceded this account of different religious traditions by asking whether the different religious traditions are so different from each other that there can be no common ground in the ways in which psychologists understand them. The account of the different religious traditions has tended to emphasize what is distinctive about each tradition. But this should not be taken to mean that there is no common ground. Here are a few salient themes that can be found common to most, though not all, religious traditions:

- spiritual reality exists, and it is important to cultivate an awareness of this, for example by prayer, study, contemplation and other practices
- the source of spiritual and material reality (God) is also the source of guidance to the right way to live (religiously-based moral and ethical injunctions); more specifically this includes –
  - justice, kindness and sexual morality should be practised in social and family relationships;
  - psychological disequilibrium can be improved by attention to one or more of the above.

SUMMARY

This chapter looked at the question of whether the psychology of religion is possible outside the Western Christian context. It is the case that the relations between psychological and religious variables differ in different cultural–religious contexts. It is also likely that some psychological measures might have different meanings in different cultural–religious contexts.

Given these provisos, it would appear that:

- there are psychological themes common to most or all religions;
- there may be particular psychological emphases and consequences in particular religious traditions;
- these psychological emphases and consequences may deserve closer psychological investigation.

3 RELIGIOUS BEHAVIOUR

This chapter will look in some detail at three areas of behaviour that are thought of as archetypically religious: *prayer, religious speech*, and *conversion*.

PRAYER, DEFINITIONS, EFFECTS AND PERCEIVED EFFECTS

Prayer is defined in the *Concise Oxford English Dictionary* as a 'solemn request or thanksgiving to God or object of worship'.

Prayer is often thought of as the most distinctive and characteristically 'religious' of all the activities that are associated with religion. Most church members say they pray regularly, and people pray more as they grow older (Brown, 1994), women may pray more often than men (Argyle and Beit-Hallahmi, 1975), and soldiers (regardless of religious affiliation) usually pray in battle and find it beneficial psychologically (Stouffer et al, 1949). It is the most frequently mentioned religious method of coping with stress (Cinnirella and Loewenthal, 1999; Loewenthal and Cinnirella, 1999a), and is widely believed to be helpful. Although some people think that prayer is only helpful if the person praying is a believer, not everyone believes that this restriction applies. And as Stouffer's work suggested, there may be few atheists in foxholes, whether the actual foxholes of the battlefield, or the metaphorical foxholes in which we cower while life's major storms rage.

---◆---

HOW PRAYER CAN HELP

'It does not matter how depressed you are, if you can divert your attention towards prayer, your problems can disappear ... giving all problems to Allah and having faith in Him is very therapeutic.'

Muslim woman, London 1997

'Remembrance of God [*dhikr Allah*] belongs to the most central activities of Sufi mystical orders ... *dhikr* can be described as partial inhibition of the ego's adaptive function – weakening of defensive functions, and an activation of the Sufi frame of reference'

Geels, 1996

'Speaking [in tongues] is a gift. Some people just say any old rubbish, they are just making it up. When you first do it, it feels like getting a tick (mark of approval) from God'

Black Christian woman, London 1997

'It [speaking in tongues] is comforting, and you feel it helps. When my child was very ill in hospital, I sat by him and spoke [in tongues] for hours, but very quietly, so that the nurses would not notice and think I was odd.'

White Christian man, London 1997

'I sometimes just walk along the street and marvel at God's creations. I feel a tremendous sense of wonder and awe.'

Jewish woman, London 1978

'Saying *tehilim* [psalms] does help. When you are tense and exhausted after a difficult day, it does help to sit and say a few psalms. You feel better, calmer, it gives you the right perspective.'

Jewish woman, London 1978

---◆---

The box of quotations above gives a flavour of the huge range of prayer experiences, as well as an idea of what the experiences usually have in common:

- *Behavioural features.* Prayer may involve behavioural preparations, like solitude from mundane distractions, seeking like-minded company, as well as bodily and postural preparations – facing in a particular direction, standing, sitting, bowing, kneeling or other kinds of special movements such as dancing.
- *Linguistic features.* The person praying uses language, perhaps a set form of words ('verbal prayer'), perhaps their own words. The speech may be aloud, or quiet, very private inner speech, or sometimes some form of seeking for inner silence ('contemplative prayer').
- *Cognitive features.* Prayer involves an orientation towards a religious or spiritual perspective on life, its purpose and meaning.
- *Emotional features.* Prayer usually provides a feeling of increased closeness to God, and perhaps support and comfort.

Types of prayer

This list of common features of prayer needs qualifying. There are different types of prayer. L.B. Brown (1994) in *The Human Side of Prayer* suggests that the most commonly understood sense of the term prayer is *petitionary*, asking for something, either for oneself or for others. But other forms of prayer may involve *thanksgiving*, also *confession* and asking for forgiveness, and of course *meditation* or contemplation. Meadow and Kahoe (1984) distinguish at least five types of prayer:

- *petitionary prayer* – the cry for help for oneself;
- *intercessory prayer* – pleading for help for another person;
- *thanksgiving* – for help and favours received;
- *adoration* – expressing awe, wonder, praise;
- *confession, dedication, communion* – righting and consolidating the relationship with God.

Meadows and Kahoe add meditation to this list, as well as distinguishing between objective prayer (focused on the object of worship) and subjective prayer (focused on the self). They also distinguish between less mature forms of prayer – expecting God to answer petitionary prayer, for example – and more mature forms of prayer – characterized by dedication and communion.

Prayer may follow a set text, or be composed spontaneously. Prayer liturgies – set forms of prayer – occur in many religions including most forms of major traditional religion. Set prayers encompass the range of types of prayer – petition, confession, contemplation – and the words are applicable to the gamut of human situations. Thus, liturgical petitionary prayer is for physical sustenance, health, peace and other universal needs.

There may be non-verbal elements, but all prayer has the common features of at least some verbal component, at least as a preliminary, and the focusing of attention onto the self in relation to the divine. The large number of definitions reviewed by Brown involves the concepts of *communication*, *union* and *closeness*.

◆

PETITIONARY AND INTERCESSORY PRAYER

Here Brown quotes from a series of 227 petitions on prayer cards from an English country church. The prayer cards were loaned by Professor Leslie Francis, and Brown comments on the 'urgency and innocence' of most of the prayers.

Please pray for:

Charlotte, a baby of 10 months who is deaf, that her hearing may be restored.

The repose of the soul of Jim. Please give consolation to his friend Greg in his loss.

My mother – in her trying times – with drink.

Me. Please take the bitterness from my heart towards my family.

My family, [that they] may soon stop arguing.

Quoted in Brown, 1994

CONFESSION AND PENITENTIAL PRAYER

Here, the person describes their failings with regret and a resolve to do better in future. Belgum (1992) writes of his childhood memories of the confessional prayer that was said in church every week:

'"We are wholly and absolutely deserving of punishment and condemnable" ... later I saw another dynamic at work. After confession one was totally forgiven ... one went from a minus ten back up to zero.'

◆

DOES PRAYER WORK?

Early scientific enquiries into this question looked at whether the things that people prayed for were more likely to happen. For example, Galton

(1883) wondered whether monarchs would be more healthy or live longer than other people because they were more likely to be prayed for. Monarchs were actually shorter-lived than other people. Galton thought that this showed that prayer is not effective. Galton also found no differences in the rate of stillbirths between praying and non-praying parents. Galton's ideas were attended to because of his scientific reputation. In fact they are not very sound, either scientifically or theologically. For instance, Galton did not look at the important question of how long monarchs live when they are *not* prayed for; his scientific method was unsound. Further, theologically, it is likely that mature prayer would involve a 'Your will, not mine' clause, indicating that the person praying would try to accept whatever happened. Moreover, Galton's studies diverted attention from the study of the conditions of use and the psychological effects of prayer.

◆

PRAYERS SAID BY WOMEN

Weissler (1998) in her study of the prayers of early modern Jewish women, offers a number of examples of the special prayers said specifically by women. For example, one prayer said while laying wicks into candles for the patriarchs and matriarchs, asks that: ' ... you may purify us of sins and trespasses. May our souls become pure (in the merit of our father Abraham) ... May [our mother Sarah] be a good advocate for us ... that our little children may not, God forbid, be taken from the world during our lives ... by Rachel's merit, God, blessed be he, will bring us back to our land, Amen. May her merit defend us, that she did not let herself be comforted until the coming of the righteous redeemer, may he come speedily and soon ... '

Weissler comments that one of the triumphs of this prayer, composed by Sarah bas Tovim, is the way it blends eschatological and domestic concerns. It pleads for purity of souls, deliverance from exile, the coming of the redeemer, but it also asks for the wherewithal to keep the children in school and marry them off, just in case the Messiah waits a little longer.

◆

An often-quoted study by Parker and St Johns (1957) was reported to show more improvement in a group of neurotic patients receiving 'prayer therapy', compared to patients receiving psychotherapy and compared to patients engaged in their normal praying habits. Again, this study is problematic. For ethical and methodological reasons, this and similar studies have not arrived at any satisfactory or reliable answer about the efficacy of prayer (Brown, 1994; Loewenthal, 1995; Wulff, 1997).

Instead of asking simply whether prayer works, we first need to ask when, why and how prayer is used, and what effect prayer is believed to have. We have seen that prayer is used for a variety of purposes (petition, contemplation, forgiveness, etc.), and there are many ideas about its psychological effects. Johnson (1956), for example, suggests the following very long and thorough list of the possible effects of prayer. It:

1. makes us aware of our needs and of realities, as we face the One who knows all, and as we examine ourselves,
2. allows confession and a sense of forgiveness as we see ourselves, but as inadequate, since self-sufficiency is self-deception,
3. engenders faith and hope that relaxes tensions, worries, and fears, and brings confidence and peace of mind,
4. puts our lives in perspective as our meditations solve problems and produce practical plans of action,
5. clarifies goals to which we can dedicate ourselves, focus our lives, and unleash latent powers to achieve,
6. renews emotional energy, through the euphoria of communication with the divine,
7. makes us responsive to the needs of other persons and channels our social and altruistic motives,
8. affirms our values and prepares us to accept whatever happens,
9. fosters our loyalty to the Ultimate and perseverance in devotion and
10. integrates our personalities through focusing upon a supreme loyalty.

WHAT IS THE EMPIRICAL EVIDENCE THAT PRAYER HAS THESE EFFECTS?

Pargament and Hahn (1986), for example, analysed American undergraduates' views of God's role in health difficulties. These undergraduates saw God as a source of support more than as moral guide. Another finding (already mentioned) is that there are indeed (almost) no atheists in foxholes. Argyle and Beit-Hallahmi (1975) reviewed studies of soldiers, who reported widespread use of prayer when in battle conditions. Stouffer (1959) reported that about 75 per cent of US army World War II veterans agreed that 'prayer had helped a lot when the going was tough'. Prayer was reported to be the most helpful of the cognitive strategies used to keep going under battle conditions, and was said to be the most helpful by those who reported being the most frightened.

Argyle and Beit-Hallahmi conclude from their review of several American studies that war experience can increase interest in religious and spiritual matters, but war veterans were often less involved with organized religion than others, and held non-orthodox views. Often, war experiences disillusioned people, so that they reported becoming less religious, but those who reported an increase in religiousness said that it was the result of the help they had experienced from the use of prayer in battle. Argyle and Beit-Hallahmi's review then supports the view that prayer has at least some of the reported psychological effects listed by Johnson.

Parker and Brown (1986), in an Australian study, included prayer as one of many possible strategies for coping with negative events and feelings. It was associated (statistically) with help-seeking behaviours. A group of clinically depressed subjects was studied on three occasions. Help-seeking (which included prayer) was not associated with improvement in depression scores. The strongest finding of this study was that self-consolatory behaviours (such as eating, drinking alcohol and spending money) were associated with a worsening of depression. This study therefore does not support the idea that prayer may be associated with an improvement in depression, but it did not look at the 'pure' effects of prayer directly.

Schatz-Uffenheimer (1993) has linked contemplative prayer in Hasidism with an emphasis on joy and a ban on sadness and regret. The essence of contemplation is focusing on unity; Schatz-Uffenheimer quotes the eighteenth-century Hasidic master, the Maggid of Mezeritch, who recommended this type of contemplation as an accompaniment to daily prayer:

> '... that there is nothing in the entire world but the Holy One, blessed be He, for the whole world is full of His glory ... that man sees himself as naught and nothing, and that his essence is only the soul that is within him, which is a portion of God above ... and there is no place empty of Him'.

More recently, scientific thinking about the effects of prayer has focused on two particular issues. First, does prayer have effects in coping with stress, and if it does, what are these effects, and how do they work? Second, instead of asking the general question whether prayer 'works', there has been some careful enquiry into questions such as *when* is prayer engaged in, for what reasons, and what effects do the 'users' of prayer *expect* – or find – it to have?

Prayer and coping with stress

Higher levels of religious involvement are normally associated with lower levels of distress and mental illness (Bergin, 1983; Levin, 1994; Loewenthal, 1995; Worthington *et al.*, 1996; Levin and Chatters, 1998). There are many reasons why this might be – better social support and belongingness among members of religious groups, and a more ordered and less severely stressful life-style are two likely reasons (Prudo *et al.*, 1984; Shams and Jackson, 1993; Loewenthal *et al.*, 1997). Some authors have suggested that religious involvement can lead to cognitive changes: McIntosh (1995), for example, thought that stress might call into play religiously-based schema which could be used to interpret unpleasant stressful events, enabling better coping and better mental health outcomes. Loewenthal, MacLeod, *et al.* (2000) showed that prayer and other religious activity was associated with reported use of religious interpretations of stress.

The beliefs and cognitions that were used more often by religiously-active people in coping with stress included the following:

- Ultimately, it is all for the best.
- Ultimately, God is in control.
- God is supporting me through this.
- Those questioned claimed a higher proportion of good (compared to unpleasant) outcomes of the stressor.

Their interpretations were in turn associated with better mental health outcomes: lower distress, anxiety and depression.

Contemplation and meditation have often been suggested to have beneficial cognitive and emotional effects (Shapiro and Walsh, 1984; Brown, 1994; Valentine and Sweet, 1999). More recent studies of prayer and meditation are better designed than earlier studies. Direction of effects can sometimes be hard to interpret, and it is hard to disentangle the effects of prayer from the other (confounded) effects of religion which are likely to have good effects – such as self-esteem, and knowing that practical help is there when needed. Nevertheless, it is hard to dismiss the fairly common-sense suggestion that prayer and contemplation affect cognition and emotion, and this in turn may have effects on mental health, and also physical health (Levin, 1994; Levin and Chatters, 1998).

Expectations about the effects of prayer

The suggestion that prayer helps by inducing thoughts (cognitions) that make the praying person feel better (emotions) may not be enough of an explanation for the believer, who sees God as a mediator, and who may see prayer as a 'magical ... trick for bypassing the laws of the universe' (to use the rather pejorative phrase of Wulff, 1997):

> My daughter ... told me that the priests in her new church worked miracles ... getting people jobs, permits ... transforming husbands from deadbeats and abusers into responsible family men, ... prostitutes into self-respecting women and wives – all through the power of faith and prayer. [She said] '... Nothing is impossible for those who believe'.
>
> (Quoted in Mathabane, 1994).

> If a man puts all his faith in God, then God will surely fulfil all his desires. No matter what is his need – whether he desires wealth, whether he desires a son – if his mind is fixed on God and he sees only God before his eyes, then automatically his wishes are granted ... When I prayed to God to release me from the army which I hated, my mind became concentrated upon Him; it became fastened upon this prayer, and so God granted his help.
>
> (Quoted in Sharma, 1971)

Wulff concedes the point made by Johnson (1953) that prayer entails a 'dynamic sense of harmony within and without, that heals conflict and loneliness'. However, the issue that is crucial for believers remains – that it is a divine response that not only 'heals conflict and loneliness', but *also* 'works miracles'.

Some psychological theorists have suggested that the most viable way of accounting for the psychological phenomena associated with religion, is to postulate the existence of God (Spero, 1992). But as stated, it has proved hard to study the effects of prayer other than by working with existing theoretical models of stress, coping, cognition and emotion. Such studies should include what the users – and non-users – of prayer believe the effects of prayer to be. A further important aim of such studies would be to look at the outcomes both of 'successful' prayers, and of disappointments, i.e. prayers for which the person praying did not get the prayed-for outcome.

For instance, many doctors and psychiatrists are concerned to know how the use of religious methods of coping interacts with other forms of help-seeking.

---------------------- ◆ ----------------------

Amy is a lively journalist in her mid-thirties. She walks very slowly, with the aid of a walking stick, and has done so since childhood, when she fell and broke her leg. 'My mother was a devout Christian Scientist, and she wouldn't take me to a doctor. She believed that prayer and faith in God were all that were needed'. Amy went along with that, and is not bitter or reproachful about her crippled status. She herself is a devout Christian Scientist. 'But I don't have the faith of my mother. I wouldn't go to a doctor for myself, but if the children had a serious medical problem, then yes I would go'.

---------------------- ◆ ----------------------

Here, prayer and faith prevented Amy's mother from seeking medical and professional help. Perhaps she felt that prayer and faith were responded to when Amy began walking again. When I met Amy, her mother was no longer alive. Amy suspected that her early-onset arthritis was connected to the fracture. She would not want to be false to her own identity and sense of Christian faith, by consulting a doctor. But her sense of commitment does not extend to her children. If they were 'very ill', or seriously injured, she would not do as her mother did. She would seek professional medical help.

Campion and Bhugra (1997) reported that in India, forty five per cent of patients visiting a modern Westernised psychiatric facility had been to see a religious healer prior to seeking help from the psychiatrists. Craissati (1990) reported that Western psychiatry is seen as a last resort in India, while religious healers are widely consulted.

The examples above were of people who first used prayer and other religious strategies, before or instead of consulting a doctor. More commonly, however, when Western medicine is readily and cheaply available, sufferers from physical and psychological illnesses will pragmatically use a mixture of medical and religious intervention. Prayer is normally the most popular method of religious intervention (Cinnirella and Loewenthal, 1999). Littlewood and Dein (1996) observed that orthodox Hasidic Jews in London would consult their doctor for illness, but seek a blessing and advice from their religious leader (Rebbe) when the illness was recalcitrant.

Figures 3.1 and 3.2 show how effective prayer was seen to be, compared with other forms of coping and treatment, for depression, schizophrenia and cancer.

Figure 3.1 Percentages agreeing that prayer, medication and psychotherapy are effective for depression and for schizophrenia (Loewenthal and Cinnirella, 1999a)

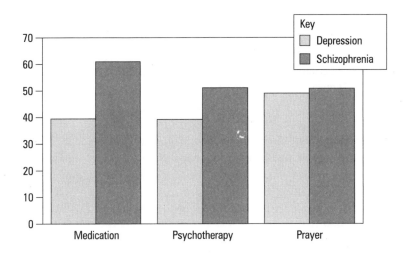

Figure 3.2 Mean ratings of the effectiveness of prayer and other methods of coping with cancer (calculated from Brown, 1994, pp 187–188)

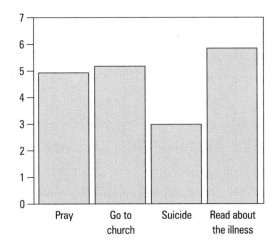

This section has suggested that it is difficult to draw sound conclusions about whether prayer really 'works' in the sense that the prayed-for effects are more likely to come about as a result of prayer. However there is much to investigate in terms of the effects of prayer upon the person praying, of the *expectations* that people have about the effects of prayer, and of the ways in which the use of prayer can affect other forms of help-seeking.

RELIGIOUS SPEECH AND LANGUAGE

Are there special properties of religious language? At one time, the term 'religious language' was used solely to denote the language used in trying to describe religious–mystical experience. It was (and still is) widely accepted that religious and mystical experiences have special properties, one of which is the clear feeling that such experience – since it is *ineffable* and *noetic* – cannot be adequately described in language (James, 1902; Jung, 1958; Stace, 1960). Thus, this type of religious language relies heavily on metaphor and simile:

> I remember one day in early spring, I was alone in the forest, lending my ear to its mysterious noises ... everything in me awoke and received a meaning. Why do I look further? He is there, without whom one cannot live. To acknowledge God and to live are one and the same thing. God is what life is.
>
> Tolstoy's experience, described in James, 1902

This type of experience is not uncommon. Although it feels as if it is stretching the resources of language, particular features (metaphor, simile) and particular contents (timelessness, spacelessness, peace, unity) tend to be recurrently reported (Hood, 1975). Mystical experience will be returned to in a later chapter. At this point we are simply concerned to draw attention to the distinctive features of the *language of mystical experience*.

There are many other types of religious discourse and text. These include:

- *Books* and other texts, *sermons* and other forms of discourse, in which a person in a position of acknowledged religious authority admonishes, informs and inspires.
- *Witnessing*, where a new member of the religious group, or a newly-inspired member, talks about their life, inspirational experiences, and the advantages of their new-found way of life which often include peace of mind, fulfilment as a person, and finding oneself.

- Converts to all religions are said to speak enthusiastically of their new-found sense of purpose, rightness, and of inner peace (James, 1902; Loewenthal, 1995; Paloutzian et al., 1999).

◆

RELIGIOUS DISCOURSE: ACKNOWLEDGED AUTHORITY

In this example, the rabbinic author suggests a cabalistic explanation for the effects of giving charity, which is thereby argued to benefit the giver:

'The essence of penitence (reuniting with God) is in the heart, since by regret from the depths of the heart one arouses the depths of the upper (spiritual) light. However to actually bring out (this light) so that it will shine (and cause effects) in the upper and lower worlds (spiritual and physical), there has to be arousal from below in the form of *action*, namely the action of charity (justice) and kindness without limit or measurement. Just as a person gives great kindness ... to one who has nothing at all ... so the Holy One blessed be He, gives his light and goodness in a manner of great kindness ... By this, all the faults in both upper and lower worlds caused by sin, are corrected.'

Rabbi Shneur Zalman of Liadi, 1973, free translation by the author

RELIGIOUS DISCOURSE: WITNESSING

Poston (1988) collected 70 testimonies of North American converts to Islam. One young mother was interviewed at the 1987 convention of the Islamic society of North America. She said that she had become frustrated with the pressures brought to bear on her by the women's liberation movement, which embodied various philosophies including equality of opportunity for women in the workplace, freedom from exploitation by men in marriage, freedom of choice regarding childbearing, and in some cases some form of sexual emancipation or liberation. She converted to Islam and married a Muslim. Her new 'traditional' life-style accorded wholly with her perception of herself as a woman. Ball in her study *Why British Women Embrace Islam* (1988) concluded that the British women converts she spoke to felt the same, as did women interviewed by Kose (1996a). This effect is not confined to Islam. Orthodox-Jewish women interviewed by Loewenthal (1988) valued the sense of purpose in their wife and mother roles. Ionescu (1998) interviewed German women converts to Japanese new religious movements. These women also appreciated the value placed on their feminine selves.

◆

- *Prophecy*, in which a person who is (now or later) agreed to have religious authority – even if it is not formally endorsed at the time – delivers messages about likely future events, often with warnings that people should improve their conduct to avert disaster.

◆

RELIGIOUS DISCOURSE: PROPHECY

In the early nineteenth century, European settlers were encroaching on more and more of Indian territory in North America. Indians had welcomed the first Europeans, but became more cautious, disillusioned and finally terrified and hostile, as Indian lands were taken by unwanted 'treaties', by force or by guile, while the Indians themselves were bought over with alcohol and cheap gifts, or deported, killed, enslaved, tortured or imprisoned to make way for the white settlers. The Indians felt spiritually tied to their lands, and they could not flourish once they were moved. One Indian leader, Tecumseh, declared 'The Great Spirit is my father. The earth is my mother'. Tecumseh said that all the land belonged to all the Indians, and that no individual tribe was empowered to sell the land or any part of it. Tecumseh at first did fight the Europeans, because he believed that if the Indians united and did not sell their land, they could hold their heritage. Meanwhile Tecumseh's brother, Tenskwatawa the Prophet, developed and spread a religion, revealed to him through trances and supernatural revelations. The Great Spirit had revealed to him that the white Americans 'grew from the scum of the great water (the Atlantic), when it was troubled by an evil spirit and the froth was driven into the woods by a strong east wind. They are numerous but I hate them. They have taken away your lands, which were not made for them.' Tenskwatawa taught that the Indians had caused their own troubles by their transgressions: adopting white ways – drunkenness, domestic animals, traders' products, guns. These corrupting influences must be thrown away, and Indians should join the religious revival and its singing and dancing. By this means, the white men would be swept away (by spiritual forces), and former conditions would be restored for the Indians.

Tecumseh and Tenskwatawa founded a religious centre, 'Prophet's Town' in Indiana, where converts lived in purity, without any of the white man's corrupting influences, while the brothers travelled, winning new converts.

Debo, 1970

◆

- *Stories*, often appearing in variant forms, which are intended to instruct, inform and inspire.

◆

RELIGIOUS DISCOURSE: STORY

A great Hasidic master, the Maggid of Mezeritch, was visited twice a year by one of his followers, Reb Zusia. One winter Reb Zusia arrived at the Maggid's house, but was told that he should return home immediately.

Reb Zusia was very taken aback. He told the Maggid that he had planned to stay for three months, to learn from him. 'I can only obey your orders if you provide me with three months' worth of inspiration.'

'Very well,' said the Maggid. 'Pay close attention to what I say now, and from it you take all the inspiration you need'.

'There are three things you can learn from a baby, and seven from a thief.

'A baby is always happy and never depressed. He is never idle. Even for a moment. And when he needs something from his father, even something insignificant, he immediately cries out.

'A thief works chiefly at night. If he doesn't obtain what he wants one night, he will try again the next. Thieves like one another, and sacrifice themselves to help each other. A thief will sacrifice himself even to obtain something insignificant. He sells what he steals for half-price, so people shouldn't know what he has. Even if he is tortured, he has one answer: "I don't know." He is proud of his work and would not change it for anything else.'

Described in Tauber, 1994

◆

Speech and the construction of reality

Psychologists and social scientists are generally interested in the way speech is used in the construction of reality, including the particular reality shared by members of a particular social group (Berger and Luckman, 1966; Potter and Wetherell, 1987). In the context of religion, we can share these same general concerns in looking at the ways in which discourse is used to shape and construct reality, including the particular reality shared by members of a particular religious group. By way of illustration, some suggestions along these lines will be reviewed.

Staples and Mauss (1987) looked at the *autobiographical discourse of converts* to Christianity and compared this to the discourse of those with a lifelong commitment. They pointed out that although autobiographies are retrospective accounts, they are actively constructed, not just verbal photographs of the past. An important function of such active construction is the reshaping of the identity of the convert. Discourse in general can be extremely important in achieving and negotiating identity (e.g. Kerby and Rae, 1998). Talking in general, and autobiographical discourse in particular, is an important part of the process of religious conversion. In William James' (1902) view, conversion turns the self into one that is 'consciously right, superior and happy' and autobiographies of religious converts often present a contrast between the current self, and a past self which was wrong, inferior and unhappy.

So witnessing – the re-telling of religious autobiography to potential converts – is important not just in persuading people of the advantages of conversion. Witnessing is important in the consolidation of identity. Poston, quoted above, suggested that women converts to Islam for example reported that since their conversion they feel they are expressing their female identity more fully. Staples and Mauss (1987) also see the telling of religious autobiographies as important in shaping and consolidating the identity of the teller.

Day (1993) has carried the constructionist view of language to its extreme point, in his examination of religious language. In his view, the language of religious belief is performative rather than informative: 'I am not saying that life is merely storied but that it is wholly so – not that we sometimes speak to convince but that we always do ... we have no way of being apart from the stories and roles and words that we know ... belief, because of its narrative components, may be viewed as a function of the audience to whom it is played'. Belief narratives, in Day's view, are used to rehearse what a person might believe, to explain belief, to justify what they do and make themselves credible. In this example, Day quotes a woman explaining what belief means to her, and justifying her church membership:

> '... For me that means you're part of a community ... it [the church] is a place where I can express my convictions ... You only know what your faith means if you practise it with other people ... I need to feel close to them and share with them what I believe ... for example, take the creed. When we say it, I feel, yes I believe that.'

Gergen (1993) suggests that this view of religious beliefs has Machiavellian implications, and to restore dignity to religious belief he suggests that belief should be seen as functioning in relationships, sometimes divisively, sometimes to bring accord.

Probably the most influential and elaborate examination of the effects of religious texts and religious discourse has been made by Sunden

(1959), in his *role theory*. In Sunden's view, religious narratives enable role-taking: religious narrative describes ways of behaving in situations with which a person can identify. The narrative 'speaks' to the person. Sunden took as his starting point the work of G.H. Mead (1934), whose work on social development was influential in sociology and social psychology. Mead said that when we have experienced a social interaction with other people, the next time a similar situation happens, we are able to *anticipate* the likely reactions of other people ... and we might adjust our own behaviour accordingly. Mead suggested an internalized *generalized other*, in some ways rather like the internalized super-ego of Freudian psychology, an inner monitor of our actions and planned actions. Many narratives offer the opportunity to widen the range of our experience, play (vicariously) new social roles, and develop new social skills. This is true for religious narratives, which enable individuals to learn to anticipate God's part in an interaction.

Glossolalia (speaking in tongues) has been understood in terms of Sunden's role theory. It is seen by the charismatic religious groups that practise it as a 'gift of the spirit'. Glossolalia has been interpreted by Holm (1987) as a pseudo-language, learned through imitation and practised according to linguistic rules, from the Bible, and from the religious community. Once an individual begins speaking in tongues, s/he has taken the 'role of baptism of the spirit'. Holm follows the observations of Samarin (1972) and Malony and Lovekin (1985) that glossolalia does not involve a special trance-like state, or other altered state of consciousness. Grady and Loewenthal (1997) noted that people who spoke in tongues did not see it as an excited or ecstatic activity, even though this was often the view of those who did not speak in tongues. It was seen as calm and calming and often carried on in private along with other activities such as cooking.

Glossolalia may sound like 'crazy talk' to those who have not heard it, and who have no knowledge of its uses in religious contexts. Littlewood and Lipsedge (1989) reported that it was quite difficult to tell whether one of their psychiatric patients was engaged in crazy talk, or was practising glossolalia. They thought she might be speaking in tongues, but her fellow church members, when called in for consultation, were clear that she was not speaking in tongues. They were sure she needed psychiatric help. Leff (1993) has drawn up useful guidelines for distinguishing between glossolalia, and *schizophrenese* – 'crazy talk' – which may be a feature of some psychotic illnesses.

- Glossolalic utterances consist of a string of phonemes which do not constitute recognizable words in any human tongue.
- Glossolalia lasts for only a few minutes.
- Glossolalia always occurs in the context of a religious ceremony and although the sounds are incomprehensible, the symbolic meaning is clear to all participants. (Author's note: there is evidence that genuine glossolalia is practiced outside formal religious ceremonies, e.g. Grady and Loewenthal, 1997).
- By contrast, in schizophrenic speech disorder, the individual words in the discourse are recognizable, but the links between them cannot be followed.
- The speech disorder of schizophrenia continues for days, weeks or longer.
- Unlike glossolalia, although the individual words are comprehensible, the overall meaning is obscure.

Leff quotes an example of disordered schizophrenic speech, which is quoted here because, like many other examples of the same kind, even though the specific meanings are not clear, the religious content is high:

> 'In my mind is a gist of something that's coming you see and to get them prepared unto on and then when the Lord is ready that gist that's back in my head when the Lord says so my Lord there's then supplied the people who who's ready to who have been applied to come in and coincide their in on the thing the Lord bringeth forth to for me to say that on that day on how and how and there and when to coincide their in unto with me.'

SOCIAL BEHAVIOUR, GROUPS AND NORMS

William James' (1902) classic understanding of religion as thoughts and feelings specific to the *individual* in their *solitude*, in relation to the divine, strikes a chord in most of us. Religion does involve inner, private feelings and experiences, which are difficult to share. Nevertheless, James has been criticized for influencing the psychology of religion too much in the direction of the study of the individual, and too little in the understanding of the social processes involved.

Individual enlightenment in Buddhism, for example, is usually sought in a monastery in which people live in closed groups, absorbing messages about how they should go about attaining enlightenment, and what they should tell themselves about what they might and should feel. Noviciates seeking enlightenment sit in rows. More experienced monks supervise the meditation and admonish – or even strike – those whose posture or appearance suggests that they are not meditating in a way which is likely to lead to success.

This example is given because we might think of meditation as a prime example of a process, which is individual, private and solitary. Nevertheless, each meditator has to be told how to meditate properly, and this is a lengthy process. It involves social interaction in structured groups, with members playing clearly defined roles.

Even a religious hermit depends on others for support, approval, freedom from molestation – in other words for validation of their identity as devoted to the solitary religious life.

So although religious experiences and feelings are private, and *may* happen – though not always – when one is alone, religion is essentially social as well as private.

A key feature of religion is the *religious group*. Like other social groups, religious groups have explicit and implicit functions, leaders, and members who play special roles, norms and standards, and ways of maintaining and developing those norms and standards. A key feature of group life is *social identity*, and Marcia (1966) has suggested that decisions about religion or other ideology are a key feature of adolescents' struggles to attain identity. Religious groups *incorporate* new members. Some religious groups do this more actively than others (Olson, 1989). In what follows, we will look at *conversion*, the incorporation of new members into a religious group, and the development of religious identity. We will also look at exiting – leaving religious groups – and at other forms of social behaviour within religious groups.

Conversion

TYPES AND MOTIFS

Would you say you have undergone any form of religious conversion? Try the following brief questionnaire:

LIVERPOOL
JOHN MOORES UNIVERSITY
AVRIL ROBARTS LRC
TITHEBARN STREET
LIVERPOOL L2 2ER
TEL. 0151 231 4022

◆

QUESTIONS ABOUT YOUR RELIGIOUS MEMBERSHIP, RELIGIOUS IDENTITY AND RELIGIOUS HISTORY

1. Do you belong to a religious group? YES/NO
2. Would you identify yourself as religious? YES/NO
3. Would you identify yourself as spiritual? YES/NO

If you said yes to any of the above, which of the following is most applicable to you?

A. I have been that way for as long as I can remember.
B. I changed quite suddenly. (Few days, hours, moments.)
C. I changed slowly and gradually. (Over weeks, months, or years.)

◆

'No' to each of the first three questions clearly disqualifies you since you do not acknowledge any religious affiliation, or religious or spiritual identity. Someone selecting option A might not be identified as a convert: Staples and Mauss (1987) would call them committed rather than converted; Scobie (1973), however, would call such a person an 'unconscious convert'. Option B describes conversion as generally understood, with a relatively clear, short turning point. If you selected option C, you might not agree that you had undergone a conversion; you might prefer to describe this as a gradual process of evaluation of options, for example. Scobie, however, called this a process of gradual conversion, claiming that it showed the crucial diagnostic feature of a shift of identity – in Scobie's study, gradual converts could point to a period in their lives when they did not (at least in retrospect) identify themselves as Christian.

Early studies of religious conversion looked at conversion to Christianity, and this interest continues. During the 1970s and 1980s, there was growing interest in conversion to the so-called 'New Religious Movements' (e.g. Buckley and Galanter, 1979; Galanter et al., 1979; Stark and Bainbridge, 1985). More recently, there have been studies of conversion and commitment to non-Christian traditional religions. (e.g. Loewenthal, 1988; Kose, 1996a, 1996b; Kose and Loewenthal, 1999; Paloutzian et al., 1999; Witztum et al., 1990b).

Conversion may be defined as affiliation with a religious group, and identification as a member. Conversion always involves an identity shift, but this can sometimes happen without very active affiliation and participation. Bragan (1977) described a young British student minister who had a fairly uneventful childhood in a dull and not particularly happy home. He had not had a religious upbringing. He had not done very well in school, and left as soon as he could, taking a series of low-skilled jobs. Meanwhile his family emigrated to New Zealand, but he decided to stay in Britain. While he was leading a lonely and aimless life in lodgings, he read a Bible, and was 'gripped' by this. He started to call himself a Christian, and the term Christian had a particular meaning for him. Eventually he joined a church and entered the ministry, but he spent a significant period identified as a Christian before belonging to a church.

Lofland and Skonovd (1981) would say that this young man's conversion history showed an 'intellectual' conversion motif. Lofland and Skonovd thought it was misleading to group conversions into *types* (as earlier writers had done), and suggested that instead most conversion histories showed a mixture of *motifs*. The intellectual motif was characterized by an exposure to religious text or discourse, followed by a shift in identity. It has been suggested that intellectual motifs are likely to increase, as books get cheaper, as televangelism increases in popularity, and (more recently) as more people have Internet access, with religious groups developing better and more attractive websites. Other conversion motifs defined by Lofland and Skonovd include the social, where friends or other social contacts first get the person involved in religious activity, the mystical, in which an otherwise unexplained mystical experience occurs and is seen to validate the religion, and experimental, in which the person tries out the religion and then makes a commitment.

◆

Mrs A is a young orthodox-Jewish mother. She had not had a religious upbringing but when she was in college she got friendly with a Jewish boy, and at Hanukah (the mid-winter festival of lights) a group of friends used to light a Menorah. The friends were all involved in the 60s-70s drug and rock counter-culture, and Mrs A said that she got a particular kick out of the juxtaposition of the traditional Menorah with the counter-culture long hair and beards of the crowd around it. She said it was 'cute'. She eventually went on to study and try out orthodox Judaism.

Described in Loewenthal, 1988

◆

Mrs A's biography shows touches of a social motif – the crowd of friends · who lit the Menorah, a mystical motif – the mild amazement and religious 'buzz' at the juxtaposition of a traditional ceremony carried out by bearers of the counter-culture, and an experimental motif, when she decided to try out Judaism 'properly'.

Kose and Loewenthal (1999) studied the conversion biographies of 70 British-born converts to Islam. These converts were likely to report experimental and intellectual motifs, and sometimes mystical and affectional motifs. Coercive and revivalist motifs were seldom reported.

A few conversions happen suddenly, but most are long drawn-out affairs (Scobie, 1975). Most people who have a religious upbringing are conscious of an often prolonged period of thought, and possibly struggle, before making some kind of conscious affirmation or commitment (Loewenthal, 1988; Marcia, 1966; Staples and Mauss, 1987; Paloutzian et al., 1999). Religious crises, doubts, defections and high points can and do occur throughout adulthood. Thus, although retrospective religious biographies often focus on a crucial turning-point, often in adolescence or early adulthood, conversion may be seen as just one (notable) feature in a life-long process.

METHODS OF CONVERSION

Religious groups have favoured and developed an enormous range of methods for attracting and incorporating new members, and for educating and retaining existing members and their children. By way of illustrating some of the variety in methods of attracting and retaining new members, two methods, those of Billy Graham and of the Moonies, are outlined in the box below.

◆

BILLY GRAHAM

This fiery North American is probably the best-known modern Christian evangelist. In the 1950s a large, efficient and apparently well-funded organization backed up his charismatic mass-meeting performances. Key features of his methods included:

- *networking* through existing church organizations to bring in large numbers of people with some interest in possible religious inspiration. Coach-loads of church members and their friends, many of whom were simply curious to see what went on, were bussed in over large distances to a mass meeting in a huge hall. Expectation and excitement built up until the appearance of the preacher, who first concentrated on ...
- *fear arousal* – everyone present was plausibly depicted as being in a state of sin and complacency. A terrifying picture was drawn of the fate that awaited all who did not regret their current ways. When terror reached its peak, the preacher offered a ray of hope. One could escape the dreaded punishments (in this world and the next) by turning to the Lord and accepting him fully into one's life ...

- *majority influence* – at this point, all those who wished to accept the Lord fully into their lives were invited to come forward, publicly signalling their (re)new(ed) commitment. Stewards then proceeded to the front of the hall to take the names and addresses of those who came forward, so that later they could be put in touch with local church organizations. To the observer in the audience, it was not clear whether those going forward were only stewards, or converts, or both. The appearance was one of a fairly eager stampede. As the rush slowed down, the preacher encouraged those still seated to come forward. Many did so, until those remaining in their seats were a minority, many of them doubtless wondering whether they were wrong to resist when so many people were going forward to make their commitment ...
- *consolidation* – stewards encouraged contacts with local churches for those who were not already involved. This lead to involvement on the social and educational fronts, and incorporation for many of those who had made a commitment at the mass meeting.

Described in Colquhoun, 1955

UNIFICATION CHURCH (MOONIES)

Probably the best-known of the post 1960s New Religious Movements, the conversion (and de-conversion) histories of members have been documented by Galanter *et al.* (1979), Barker (1984), Bromley and Shupe (1979) and others. Long and Hadden (1983) suggested that the Moonies' conversion methods developed throughout the 1970s, until they were quite effective at gaining and incorporating new members, although they were less effective in retaining members.

- *initial contact with unattached* – potential new members would be identified in public places by features like their youth, and not being in a hurry. A member would engage the potential recruit in conversation on a plausible pretext like offering something for sale or asking the time. As the conversation developed, the potential recruit would be offered friendship or possibly the hope of a sexual or romantic involvement. The potential recruit would be invited back to 'my place', which proved to be the crowded communal dwelling of many Moonies. There was often initial disappointment that an intimate encounter was not going to happen, but this disappointment dissipated under the impact of so-called ...
- *love-bombing* – a meal would be served and the new recruit would feel overwhelmed and impressed by the affection and esteem offered by the new friends. Thereafter s/he would report that they 'always seemed to be running into' one or more of these new friends. The recruit would be invited round again, and eventually invited to a country retreat, where ...
- *incorporation* would continue – isolated from other social ties (work, family, friends – no telephone or letters) and from other sources of information (television, newspapers, radio) the new member would join in group rituals and be taught secret doctrines of the group.

◆

One popular social-scientific distinction is between established *church-es* and newly-developing *sects* or other new religious groups (Wilson, 1970). An alternative – though similar – distinction is between 'low-tension' and 'high-tension' religious groups (Pope, 1942; Bainbridge, 1997). High-tension groups, by contrast with low-tension groups:

- renounce wider society and culture;
- feel persecuted;
- do not co-operate with established religion;
- do not value property, but value poverty;
- emphasize evangelism and conversion.

Olson (1989) was able to show that members of older established religious groups were less friendly to outsiders and less interested in new members than were members of new religious groups. Newer groups 'needed' new members. So conversion and incorporation methods *vary* with the age, size and other features of the religious group. Other features that might affect conversion and incorporation methods include Glock and Stark's (1965) suggestion that different perceived deprivations or needs are met by different types of religious group. For example, cults are suggested as meeting psychic needs, i.e. needs for exciting or notable religious or spiritual experiences. Cults are generally closed, high-tension religious groups, characterized by a charismatic leader, who demands economic and other surrender, including the giving up of other social ties (Paloutzian, 1983, 1996).

Bainbridge (1997) has described the process of 'implosion', in which members of a new (religious) group come to be more dependent on each other, and sever their ties with the wider social network, creating the conditions for beliefs and practices which are not tied to the norms of wider society. In return for any loss or sacrifice, members learn 'secret' teachings and are offered special mystical or religious experiences in the context of a supportive and cohesive group. Buckley and Galanter (1979), for example, reported that 'light' was often seen by potential new recruits to the Divine Light Mission, a cult led by the very youthful Guru Maharaj Ji. Potential recruits would be invited to meetings in which members would 'deliver satsang' – accounts of their own religious experiences. New recruits might experience light and warmth, which would be seen as a validation of the truth of the accounts they were listening to. Subsequent incorporation into the group involved feelings of acceptance by other members, purpose in life, and the regular practice of meditation which (temporarily at least) gave feelings of peace.

ARE SOME KINDS OF PEOPLE MORE LIKELY THAN OTHERS TO BECOME CONVERTS?

Having seen that religious groups may vary in how much they 'need' new members, and in how they go about recruiting them, if they recruit at all, we now ask whether some kinds of people are more likely than others to seek religious experience, to become a cult victim or target, or to become a convert to a more traditional religion.

Have you encountered any of the following views of converts? Do you share any of these views? Converts are:

- weak-minded;
- unstable personalities;
- easily led.

Is there truth in any of these views? Ullman (1982) studied converts and lifelong adherents in four religious groups, two traditional and two 'new'. The converts reported more unhappiness and stress (in the pre-conversion period) than did the lifelong adherents, and they also reported a more difficult relationship with their fathers. Several other authors have reported a period of unhappiness, doubt or searching among converts, in the pre-conversion period (Bragan, 1977; Brown, Spilka and Cassidy, 1978; Clark, 1979). There is anecdotal evidence that some religious groups seeking converts may actively target those who are unattached or have undergone a crisis, for example by visiting the relatives of those reporting deaths of close family members in the local newspaper. However, Heirich (1977) and Batson et al. (1993) have suggested that the evidence of a pre-conversion period of stress or unhappiness is unclear and difficult to interpret.

In general, there has been a large amount written on religious conversion and personality change. This has recently been reviewed by Paloutzian, Richardson and Rambo (1998). They concluded that conversion had minimal effects on the elemental personality functions (character, and the so-called 'Big Five' personality traits), but that 'it can result in profound life-transforming changes in the mid-level functions such as goals, feelings, attitudes and behaviours, and in the more self-defining personality functions such as identity and life meaning'.

A very interesting hypothesis about conversion was put forward by Kirkpatrick (Kirkpatrick and Shaver, 1990; Kirkpatrick, 1992). Kirkpatrick suggested that the individual relationship with God might reflect styles of relationship developed in infancy and early childhood. If this sounds like a re-invention of the Freudian hypothesis about God resembling the father-figure, it is not. Kirkpatrick's hypothesis is based on Bowlby's attachment theory (1969, 1973, 1980) which is based on observations of infants with their adult caretakers, usually their mothers. Bowlby suggested three *attachment styles*:

- *secure*, in which the caretaker is a base, returned to when there are threats. In the absence of danger, the child leaves base to explore and play freely;
- *anxious-avoidant*, in which the child is nervous and clingy, reluctant to let go and explore, and in which the adult may show signs of rejection. Causality is difficult to determine since the child's clinging may be a response to rejection and insecurity, while the adult avoidance may be a response to excessive demands for holding and comfort from the child;
- *mixed*, in which both secure and anxious-avoidant styles are evident.

Kirkpatrick's idea is that attachment styles transfer into the religious situation, and thus a person's relationship with God is similar in style to their relationship with their primary caregiver. Further, Kirkpatrick has shown that those who reported a secure attachment style were more likely to follow the religious path of their primary caregiver than those who were insecurely attached. Thus, those with devout mothers were likely to be devout, and those with irreligious mothers were likely to be irreligious. The securely attached reported a less intense religious relationship, while those with an anxious-avoidant style were likely (if religious) to have undergone intense experiences, and to have a more intense relationship with God.

This ties in with earlier research reports that there were a number of features sometimes found to distinguish those who have undergone a *sudden* conversion experience, from those who have not. The latter includes those who are not religious, as well as those who have undergone gradual conversion, and lifelong religious adherents. Compared to gradual converts, lifelong religious and non-religious, sudden converts have been reported to be more dogmatic, but happier (since conversion) (Stanley, 1964; Shaver *et al.*, 1980).

There have been mixed reports regarding anxiety and psychopathology among converts. There have been few really adequate prospective studies, in which people are followed longitudinally and interviewed at intervals. Witztum *et al.* (1990b) reported one such study, which showed evidence of a 'honeymoon effect'. A pre-conversion period of stress and distress was followed by a post-conversion 'honeymoon', which was followed by a drop in well-being as the convert tries to come to terms with the demands of long-term adjustment. Other, non-longitudinal studies are generally consistent with this picture (Loewenthal, 1995).

So where does this leave us with respect to the question with which we started this section? Are certain kinds of people conversion-prone? There is no satisfactory evidence allowing a firm answer. But we have seen that it is possible that some religious groups may actively target some kinds of people, those who are likely to be unattached, and/or under stress. We have also seen that conversion may produce a transient rise in well-being, which may make conversion attractive to the unhappy or discontented. Finally, we have seen the suggestion that *sudden* conversion may be associated with a particular style of personal adjustment.

TWO SOCIAL-PSYCHOLOGICAL PERSPECTIVES ON CONVERSION

Religious conversion is a complex process, and several ways in which psychologists have considered it have been discussed. Here, in a little more depth, are two contrasting psychological approaches.

Conversion and identity: One psychologist who encouraged the study of life-long development was Erikson (1963). In his psycho-social theory of personality development, he argued the case for societal influence in the development of personality. He suggested that we can never stand still, since life presents a continual series of challenges. Erikson called them developmental tasks, and there are characteristic developmental tasks for each stage of life. Erikson identified eight such stages, and described patterns of personality organization characteristic of success and failure in negotiating each stage. One developmental task is the development of identity, which normally takes place in late adolescence/early adulthood. Marcia (1966) suggested that identity is chiefly based on *occupation* and *ideology*. In a series of interviews with young men in college (in the USA), he observed four possible states vis-à-vis the development of identity:

- *foreclosed*, in which the person has gone along with the roles and beliefs that seemed to be expected of him by his family. They are confident about what they believe and what they are likely to do in life, and have not had to put much thought into these decisions;

LIVERPOOL JOHN MOORES UNIVERSITY
LEARNING SERVICES

- *achieved*, in which the person has achieved an identity – beliefs and an (intended) occupation in life – but was aware of a period of decision-making;
- *moratorium*, in which the person is hoping to settle on an identity but is still in the process of exploring and deciding;
- *diffused*, in which the person has given up, or never embarked, on the process of forming an identity. The identity-diffused person is likely to be cynical or hopeless about identity – no path is ever likely to be worthwhile, and they see themselves as unlikely ever to want to make any kind of commitment.

Measures based on this scheme have been used in the study of religious development. Thus Watson *et al.* (1998) showed that individuals who were high on intrinsic religiosity were more likely to report identity achievement compared to other people. Intrinsic religiosity is regarded as a sincere style of religious orientation, and is defined and discussed more fully in chapter 6. Beit-Hallahmi (1989) has suggested that all religions aim to create members with a high level of ego-involvement, with a strong religious identity. However only a minority may actually achieve this level of involvement.

Moscovici and minority influence: In 1980 the social psychologist Serge Moscovici wrote a paper called 'Towards a theory of conversion behaviour' suggesting that some of the processes he had observed when people in small groups changed their minds, might be at work in the formation of religious movements, as well as in processes like the acceptance of new scientific theories.

Early social-psychological work on social influence in groups had been greatly affected by Asch's (1955) seminal work on compliance and conformity. Asch looked at situations in which most members of a group expressed an opinion that was at variance with the truth. Very often, the reluctant minority went along with the majority, even though this was usually only outward compliance. They expressed reservations about the majority view, but went along with the majority opinion so as 'not to mess things up', a phenomenom similar to the one vividly described by Janis (1982) as 'groupthink'. Moscovici suggested that when people appear to change their minds under majority influence, there is little inner conviction. So under what circumstances does inner conviction arise, as in religious conversion and the development of new movements in religions? Moscovici suggested that conviction might come after persuasion by *minority* influence, a situation in which even just one person argues for an innovative point of view, with sincerity and *consistency*. Later social psychological work has confirmed the importance of consistency in minority influence (Van Avermaet, 1996) but there seems to have been little or no examination of Moscovici's suggestions as applied specifically to religious conversion – even though there is every tantalizing indication that the cap might fit very well.

Exiting religious groups

How, when and why might members leave religious groups? What are the consequences of defection or exiting? These questions have been looked at less often than the questions of how, when and why people join religious groups. But they have been investigated.

For example, Jacobs (1987) has proposed a two-stage descriptive model of individual disaffiliation from cult-like religious movements. She suggests that members first loosen bonds with other members, and then become disenchanted with and disengaged from the charismatic leader.

Jill Mytton (1992) has described some aspects of the aftermath of defection from a closed religious group in Britain. Feelings of guilt about the defection, and isolation, were partly explained by the fact that ex-members were ostracized by their former friends from within the group, who were not permitted to have any more dealings with the defector. This prohibition can even extend to members of the same family. Somewhat similarly, Mordechai (1992) describes how members of her family were ostracized by a close-knit religious group – indeed, excluded – for apparently quite minor deviations from the wishes of the group leader.

Another study of ex-members involved a different scenario. The Rajneeshpuram commune was on an isolated farm, and members had limited contact with the outside world. Following a disbanding of the commune, many members kept up some involvement with the Rajneeshee movement. In a study, by Latkin (1993), there were few signs of psychological distress following disaffiliation. However, in this study, the scenario was not one of individual disenchantment, but of a 'mass exodus', for reasons not clearly specified. Latkin thought these ex-members were coping well, but their disaffiliation may not have been complete. Although their commune had disbanded, most kept up the Rajneeshee clothing and name, and maintained contact with other members.

Many religious groups have been depicted unsympathetically, probably particularly so when the group is 'closed' and does not welcome contact between members and the 'outside world'. It is likely that at least some members of some religious groups do behave abusively or exploitatively – even though apologists will say that abuse should not happen. It is likely that abuse in its various unpleasant forms may play a role in causing defection from religious groups (e.g. Biale, 1983). But people may stay in religious groups and continue to endure abuse, just as in other abusive situations, simply because they do not have anywhere to escape to. And people may leave religious groups – especially 'low-tension', open groups – for quite mild reasons, if they find something better to do.

◆

A British couple married in church. The husband did not see himself as religious but he saw that the religious vows meant something to his wife and he wanted to please her, saying that it was important to her to have the shared experience in the church wedding. The husband also conceded that it was important for the children to have a grounding in faith and so he attended church with the family when the children were young. When they grew older, he felt uncomfortable and hypocritical in the church services, for example saying the creed. While his wife went to church, he began to spend the time going for solitary walks or reading.

Described in Day, 1993

◆

The husband in Day's example found the church services boring and meaningless, and appeared to have no significant religious interests outside the church context.

Call it what you will: defection, exiting, de-conversion ... leaving religion does not seem to be a popular topic for study by psychologists, even though 'secularization' has been an important topic for sociologists. These topics are scarcely referred to in books on the psychology of religion, so although we have some understanding of the social conditions associated with a decline in religious practice, we have only a few scattered clues about the psychological processes involved, and their psychological implications.

Other types of religious behaviour

Many other kinds of behaviour are important in religion, including those used to maintain the values and norms of religious groups. These range from favoured methods of dressing and proclaiming identity, through to education and all the various forms of child-rearing favoured or encouraged in religious groups, including forms of sanction and encouragement that are used by adult members. We know very little about the psychological aspects of these. There has been little attention given, for example, to the question of whether there are systematic effects of religion on methods of child-rearing (Capps, 1994; Loewenthal, 1995).

There is also the question of whether and how religions are associated with the encouraging or discouraging of particular forms of behaviour. For example, helpfulness, kindness, and the practice of charity have all received much attention in religious texts. Are religious people really more helpful than others? We return to these questions in chapter six.

SUMMARY

This chapter looked at psychologists' approaches to religious behaviour. Prayer, religious speech and language, and group behaviour (particularly conversion processes) were examined. Finally, some aspects of leaving religious groups were examined.

Prayer is probably the most distinctively religious of all forms of behaviour, and is widely believed to be helpful. Types of prayer were examined and their uses, effects and perceived effects.

The use of language in religious contexts was examined: the language of mystical experience, sermons, prophecy, stories, and witnessing. Two important functions of religious language are the setting up of role models (as in Sunden's role theory), and the use of language in recounting personal religious biography, which develops, defines and consolidates self-perception and identity.

Group behaviour was examined with particular reference to the processes involved in religious conversion, and a number of studies and theories were described. Finally, brief mention was made of other kinds of religious behaviour.

4 RELIGIOUS THOUGHTS

In this chapter we will examine religious belief, its definition and measurement. Qualitative and quantitative studies of religious belief will be described. We will look at work on changes in religious belief over the life-span, including faith development.

RELIGIOUS BELIEF

Religious behaviour and religious belief are clearly different things (Brown, 1987). How many times have you heard somebody claim something like:

'I go through all the motions, but it doesn't mean anything',
or
'I just go along to services to please my family. I'm not a believer',
or, conversely
'I can believe without having to go to church'?

Empirically, religious behaviour and belief may tend to go along together. Those who are more religiously active are more likely to believe. But this does not mean that we can tell what is in a person's mind from knowing how they behave.

Behaviour and belief require separate study. They do affect each other. They may be inter-related, but they are different types of human activity, with different antecedents. So we turn from religious behaviour to the cognitive aspects of religion – beliefs.

The term *religious belief* will be used here to refer to the *content* of beliefs about religious matters – *what* the individual believes about God, spirituality and related matters.

One way of looking at the content of beliefs is to ask people about their beliefs, and to record what is said. Researchers who have used this qualitative approach include Rizzuto (1974, 1979) and Fowler (1981). Rizzuto used clinical interviews to assess how individuals conceived of God, and to examine how the concept of God related to experiences in family life, especially during childhood. Fowler used extended interviews to look at what people believed, how they justified their beliefs, and how faith – defined in a broad sense – developed throughout adulthood. Some of Fowler's findings will be described in this chapter, while Rizzuto's work, which focuses more strongly on the *feelings* involved in religious ideas, will be described in the next chapter.

Psychologists and social scientists have also tried to quantify beliefs. For example, Table 4.1 shows the percentages of believers in different Christian concepts, in three different Christian denominations in Australia in the late 1960s.

There are several interesting things in this table. First, even a 'fundamental' item of religious belief – believing in God – was not held by quite large numbers of people who claimed affiliation with a religious group ... 10 per cent plus for the Protestant denominations. Second, there were a lot of Protestants, over 30 per cent, who did not believe in heaven, and most Protestants – over 70 per cent – did not believe in hell. Information like this can be used in several interesting ways. For example, we can compare such information across denominations and religious or cultural groups – as in Table 4.1 – or at different points in time. This gives useful pointers as to the social conditions associated with variations in belief.

Another way of quantifying beliefs involves the semantic differential, which is a kind of rating scale developed by Osgood *et al.* (1957). The box on p.60 shows a simple example.

Table 4.1 Percentages of believers in different Christian concepts (based on Brown, 1987)

	Anglican	Roman Catholic	Methodist
God	88	94	90
Heaven	60	82	70
Hell	26	64	28

---◆---

SEMANTIC DIFFERENTIAL RATING

Mark an × on each line to show how you would locate the meaning of each word:
God is

GOOD ——————————————— BAD
STRONG ——————————————— WEAK

Heaven is

GOOD ——————————————— BAD
STRONG ——————————————— WEAK

Hell is

GOOD ——————————————— BAD
STRONG ——————————————— WEAK

from Osgood et al. 1957

---◆---

Osgood *et al.* asked large numbers of people to rate large numbers of words on large numbers of semantic differential scales. Statistical analysis (factor analysis) suggested that there were three main factors underlying meaning – at least, meaning as it was being assessed using this measurement method. These three factors were *evaluation*, *potency*, and *activity*. Snyder and Osgood (1969) published a semantic atlas, giving the profiles of a number of words. Brown suggests that most 'familiar religious concepts (mostly Christian) draw high evaluation and potency scores'. Table 4.2 shows the evaluation and potency scores for the three words from Table 4.1 and Figure 4.1. The highest possible positive score would be +3, and the most extreme possible negative, –3. God is seen as mildly but not markedly pleasant, heaven as very pleasant, and hell as (unsurprisingly) unpleasant. All three concepts are high on potency. By way of comparison, Christians (to the North American Christians making the ratings) were seen as pleasant and potent, while atheists were seen as somewhat unpleasant and – would you have guessed this? – impotent.

You might look at this information and think 'So what? We all know that heaven is supposed to be a nicer place than hell, so why do we need major surveys to tell us that most people think this?' The first response to such a complaint is that we can never be sure that people believe what we think they believe. This kind of information is interesting for other reasons. As with the information in Table 4.1, we can compare information collected at different times, or from different groups of people, to

Table 4.2   Semantic differential factor scores for five religious concepts (adapted from Brown, 1987; Snyder and Osgood, 1969)

	Evaluation	Potency
God	+0.43	+2.43
Heaven	+2.55	+2.47
Hell	-2.09	+1.93
Christians	+2.11	+1.90
Atheists	-0.93	-0.53

get clues about the social conditions that are associated with different kinds of belief. It is also interesting to *compare* the information in Tables 4.1. and 4.2. This might give clues about the psychological dynamics underlying beliefs. I wondered for instance whether hell was an unpopular belief because it is seen as both unpleasant *and* powerful. If I do not believe in it, perhaps that weakens its power. Perhaps if I refuse to believe in it, it might be less likely to get me?

There are more elaborate ways of looking at beliefs and their structure and their nature. One popular technique among psychologists is the *repertory grid*. This is a method of studying *individual* systems of beliefs and values, *construct systems*, developed by Kelly in the 1950s (Kelly, 1955). Constructs can be defined as the key concepts and values used by the individual to construe and organize their world, and regulate their lives and social relationships.

To give an idea of how a repertory grid is developed, imagine or carry out the following:

- First take about a dozen pieces of paper, and write on each piece of paper the name of a significant person. The list might be something like:

Mother	Liked aunt or uncle
Father	Disliked aunt or uncle
Liked Teacher	Best friend
Disliked teacher	A friend
Grandmother	Disliked person
Grandfather	Doctor

- Fold the papers, then pull out any three, and open them. Write down *one* respect in which any two of them are *alike*, and in which they differ from the third. Fold the papers and put them back in the 'pool', and pull out a further three. This might include one or two of a previous selection, and this does not matter.
- Again write down a respect in which any two resemble each other and differ from the third. Repeat this until the same sorts of ideas (called personal constructs) begin to come up over and over again.
- There are several ways of using this information. One might be to construct a repertory grid, in which a person would be able to show how different concepts fit into his or her own personal construct system. Table 4.3 shows a hypothetical repertory grid.

The grid can be completed by writing a number from say 1 to 10 to show the extent to which each concept in the top row displayed each construct (from the vertical column). Thus, if I think that God is very kind, I might put 9 or 10; if I think God is heartless, I might put 1 or 2.

O'Connor (1983) has used repertory grid methods to study religious concepts and values. O'Connor's work, in Australia, compared non-religious participants with committed Roman Catholic priests and sisters. Religiously committed participants were found to include more constructs and elements in their grids than did non-religious participants. The religious participants included fewer elements from their immediate families and more from authorities, which one would expect given the required life-style of Catholic priests and sisters. Religious participants included more constructs to do with the feelings and behaviour of others towards the subject. This study does show some important effects of a religious life-style upon cognition; in this case the differences are what might be expected from our knowledge that Catholic priests and sisters do not found families of their own.

Table 4.3   A hypothetical repertory grid

Construct	God	Heaven	Hell	Christian	Atheist
Kind (versus heartless)	9	9	1	.	.
Intelligent (versus stupid)	.	.	.		
Lively (versus dull)	.	.	.		
Friendly (versus snobbish)	.	.	.		

Brown (in preparation) is using somewhat similar methods, also based on Kelly, to look at beliefs and how these fare under different forms of stress. One might suspect that stressful events can have a shattering, or a strengthening and enriching effect upon beliefs, but which beliefs are most likely to be affected? By which kinds of crises would they be most affected? And what exactly happens when a belief is shattered, or enriched, or otherwise changed? The work of Allport (1950) and others on war veterans (Argyle and Beit-Hallahmi, 1975) has shown some ways in which stress could affect beliefs and cognitions, but Brown's is the first research to look at this in detail. Brown's participants are asked for a detailed list of beliefs held in various contexts, and a detailed study is being made about how the importance, uses and contents of these beliefs are affected by crises of various kinds, including burglary and chronic illness.

So far we have looked at work on religious ideas that has involved quite simple practical methods of study, usually yielding *numbers*. The work I have described does indicate the variety and complexity of religious ideas, but only to a limited extent. Very often, the focus has been on making comparisons between different groups of people, or people in different situations, in order to study the effects of social circumstances upon religious concepts. Quantitative methods are very useful for this kind of endeavour.

We turn next to look at the kind of work on religious beliefs and concepts of God that has mainly been non-quantitative. This work has indicated in greater depth some of the variety and complexity of religious ideas. Much of it has been focused on the questions of how and why the nature of religious belief, and the concept of God, changes over the life-span.

CHANGES IN RELIGIOUS BELIEF OVER THE LIFE-SPAN

One of several early studies on children's religious concepts, and how these change with development, was carried out by Thun (1959). He conducted discussions with schoolchildren on questions like the experience of death, heaven, hell and other religious topics. The children participated enthusiastically. In his work with six to eleven-year-olds, Thun identified several features of childhood religion:

1. *Readiness.* Not only did the children participate enthusiastically, Thun thought they had a spontaneous disposition to think about religious issues without special prompting.

2. *Capacity for mystical experience*, especially in church.
3. *Dependence on environment*. Children's ideas were influenced by their environment, for example whether they were city or country dwellers, and by media and other input.
4. *Limitation*. Children's religious thinking tended to be magical, anthropomorphic, egocentric and realistic.
5. *Changeableness*. Children's religious ideas are changeable, leading either to more mature ideas, defensively-held beliefs, or religious indifference.

Thun highlighted some major features of the quality of children's religious thinking.

Goldman (1964) pioneered a more detailed examination of changes in the quality of children's religious thinking. Goldman was particularly interested in the observation that adolescents may think of religious beliefs as childish and naive. Goldman's approach built on some fundamental ideas introduced by Piaget.

Piaget

The best-known and possibly most fundamental of stage-developmental theories of cognitive development is Piaget's (e.g. Piaget, 1967). Prior to Piaget, the development of thinking was said to have been thought of as a series of successively more polished and accurate versions of adult thought. Piaget showed that children's thinking was radically and qualitatively different from that of adults. Briefly, Piaget's controversial view of cognitive development involves a series of stages unfolding from each other:

1. *Pre-operational thinking*. In early infant development, thinking is concentrated on the infant's sensory impressions and motor movements in the here-and-now. 'Schemata' (schematized memories, images, plans of action) are built up. In early childhood, the beginnings of symbolic thought appear, in the form of words and play for example.
2. *Concrete operational thinking*. From about the age of six the child becomes capable of elementary logical operations and manipulations of things in relation to each other. However, these manipulations are not, Piaget claims, at an abstract level. The child's thinking is no longer dominated by immediate sensory impressions. A classic demonstration of the transition from pre-operational to operational thinking is to ask a child in the five to seven age-range to make two

balls of plasticine of exactly the same size. One ball is then rolled out into a long string and the child is then asked if the two pieces of plasticine are the same. Younger children will reply: 'No – that one is bigger' (this might be either piece, the longer or the fatter one, depending on whether length or width has caught the child's attention). Older children will reply without hesitation, as do adults, that they are still the same, the same amount of plasticine. Children in transition will show some hesitation, and will often announce the mature, conservation-of-quantity response with some excitement: 'No – yes – it's still the same, it looks different but – it isn't'.

3. *Formal operational thinking.* From around the age of eleven onwards there is increasing ability to undertake abstract logical operations. A simple example: John is taller than Michael. David is taller than John. Who is taller, Michael or David? Formal operational thinking increases in type, sophistication and power with age, but is essential to deal with even a relatively simple question like the relative heights of Michael and David.

In essence Piaget showed how thinking shifted from the concrete, sensory-input dominated mode of early childhood, to the more abstract modes of adulthood. Piaget's work has stimulated a number of distinguished cognitive-developmental psychologists, who have both criticized aspects of Piaget's work, and elaborated on the foundations established (e.g. Donaldson, 1978). Piaget himself made some attempt to relate stages in the development of operational thinking to religious thought, as did a number of Piagetians (Elkind, 1964, 1971). We shall concentrate here on Goldman and his interest in the adolescent view of religion as childish and naive.

Goldman

Goldman (1964) looked at religious thinking from childhood to adolescence, concentrating on children's understanding of biblical narrative and the theology taught in school-time compulsory religious instruction. Goldman thought that children developed a concrete understanding of biblical material and metaphor, and this interfered with a more sophisticated interpretation of the material when it was encountered in adolescence. Thus, a metaphor such as the 'Heavenly Father' might be interpreted anthropomorphically by young children, in terms of something like a human form in the sky – the 'old man in the sky', subject-matter of traditional religious paintings, and indeed modern advertising, for example, the advertisement for the (British) National Lottery which features a heavenly finger pointing from the sky, along with the message that 'It could be you'. Goldman thought that when adolescents encounter religious material, narratives, metaphors and messages, they can be blinkered by their over-concrete earlier interpretations, developed when they were young children. Goldman suggested that unless religious educators encourage search, questioning and exploration, rather than teaching infallible truths, adolescents are likely to reject religious messages as babyish and not adapted to their experience and understanding.

Oser and Gmunder (1991) developed the cognitive-developmental study of religious ideas, proposing a 'Double Helix' five-stage model for the development of religious thinking. Other ideas about religious development were put forward by Meadow and Kahoe (1984). Their scheme has an attractive, common sense appeal. They propose that children are first motivated to engage in religious activity by *extrinsic* factors. The child proceeds to a stage of religious observance which is socially-controlled: beliefs and behaviour are tied to group standards. Following this, an internalized, *intrinsic* religion can be developed, followed by autonomous religion which involves a more questioning, *questing* approach. Paloutzian (1996) has pointed out that there are no developmental studies of extrinsic, intrinsic and quest religiosity (orientations to religion which are discussed more fully in chapter 6), so we have no evidence of any support for Meadow and Kahoe's proposal. Fowler (1981) was also interested in the development of religious thinking, but he was also interested in social and moral development as well. Fowler was interested in faith, both religious faith, and faith in a broader sense of the term, and his work will be discussed in the next section. Paloutzian (1996) offers a good review and discussion of several theories of religious development.

RELIGIOUS FAITH AND ITS DEVELOPMENT

What is faith? Is it a culturally limited concept? How does faith differ from religious belief? One might want to say that the two concepts are so similar that it is not worthwhile to try and distinguish them. In everyday language, a religious 'believer' would be expected to 'have' religious faith. Here, however, we will use the term *belief* to refer to *content*, while the term *faith* will be used to denote a particular cluster of beliefs and emotions, generally summarized by feelings of trust that God will somehow enable the individual to bear life's trials, which somehow have some purpose even if not at all obvious. This departs from more general definitions such as that offered by Smith (1979) who defines faith as 'one's orientation or total response to oneself, others and the universe ... [reflecting] the human capacity to see, to feel, to act in terms of a transcendent dimension' (quoted by Wulff, 1997).

Nevertheless, here I have chosen to be more specific, and distinguish between religious belief and religious faith.

One way of operationalizing faith might be through assessing it through a simple measure, such as Maton's (1989) spiritual support scale (see box).

SPIRITUAL SUPPORT SCALE

Next to each of the statements below indicate how accurately the statement describes your experience, using number from 1 (not at all accurate) to 5 (completely, always true):

1. I experience God's love and caring on a regular basis.
2. I experience a close personal relationship with God.
3. Religious faith has not been central to my coping.

Maton, 1989

However, many commentators have suggested that the quality of faith varies between different people, and changes as a result of experience and development.

Fowler (1981) studied faith using open-ended interviews. He was interested in linking religious faith to theories of cognitive development. Fowler based his scheme of faith development on three separate strands in stage-developmental theory: the psycho-social, the cognitive, and the moral, taking particularly into account the work of Erikson (1963), Piaget (e.g. 1967) and Kohlberg (e.g. 1968, 1969). Erikson deals with psycho-social development from a psychoanalytical perspective, Piaget deals with cognitive development, as just described, and Kohlberg deals with moral development. Before saying more about Fowler, we should briefly describe the important views of Erikson and of Kohlberg (Piaget's work has already been outlined in this chapter).

Erikson

Erikson had a psychoanalytic training, and he became interested in the way culture structures transitions through fairly universal stages, in infancy, childhood, adolescence, young adulthood, middle age, and old age. Erikson's psycho-social stage-developmental theory takes us through the crises characteristic of seven stages in the life-span. Erikson suggested that the individual who successfully resolves the crises inherent in each stage will go on to face the dilemmas of the next stage. Those who are not successful will remain locked, as it were, into that feature of character. Table 4.4 shows an outline of Erikson's psycho-social stages, and their outcomes in terms of character. Thus, for example in very early infancy, the infant who receives 'good-enough' care-taking (to borrow Winnicott's (1958) famous term) will develop 'basic trust'. A number of commentators including Fowler have pointed to the importance of this and other features of Erikson's theory for religious development. Erikson himself was deeply interested in religious issues, writing psycho-biographies of the eminent religious leaders Luther and Gandhi.

Kohlberg

Kohlberg's (1968, 1969) account of moral development was the third important foundation of Fowler's approach to understanding the development of faith. Kohlberg's theories have waxed and waned in popularity and influence, but they have been generally judged as the single most

Table 4.4 A brief summary of Erikson's psycho-social stage-developmental theory

Stage	Age (approximate)	Successful resolution	Unsuccessful resolution
Trust – mistrust	<1	Hope	Fear
Autonomy – shame	1–3	Will-power	Self-doubt
Initiative – guilt	4–5	Purpose	Unworthiness
Industry – inferiority	6–11	Competency	Incompetency
Ego identity– role confusion	12–20	Fidelity	Uncertainty
Intimacy – isolation	21–24	Love	Promiscuity
Generativity – stagnation	25–65	Care	Selfishness
Ego integrity – despair	66+	Wisdom	Meaninglessness

important contribution to the understanding of moral thought. Kohlberg founded his approach on Piagetian stage-developmental principles. Piaget had explored moral development, but had only examined changes in the quality of moral thought during childhood. Kohlberg argued that moral thinking can continue to change and develop throughout adolescence and adulthood, and he examined this via interviews and discussions with adolescents and adults. The material under discussion was a difficult moral dilemma (for example, see box).

A man's wife was dying from a rare illness. He discovered that a pharmaceutical researcher with his laboratory in the same city had developed a medication that was successful in treating this illness. The medication was extremely expensive. The man went to his bank, his friends and relatives and borrowed all the money he possibly could. He then went to the pharmaceutical researcher and asked for a supply of the drug, promising that he would pay off the outstanding amount as soon as possible. The pharmaceutical researcher refused to supply the drug. Meanwhile the man's wife was near death. What should the man do? Should he try to steal the drug?

Described in Rest, 1979

Kohlberg observed that people's proposed solutions, and the reasons they gave for them, varied. Kohlberg proposed *three* broad levels in moral development, each subdivided into two stages (Kohlberg later proposed a seventh stage). Briefly, Kohlberg's three levels are:

1. *Pre-conventional* – where actions are only judged in terms of the consequences for the self. For example, 'He should steal the drug because otherwise he will get into trouble for letting his wife die'. Or, 'He shouldn't steal the drug because he will be sent to prison for stealing'.
2. *Conventional* – actions are judged in terms of the anticipated judgement of others, or existing rules or laws of society. 'He should not steal the drug because stealing is not right, or is against the law', or 'He should steal the drug because it would be wrong to let his wife die'. At this level, the person will no longer be self-centred; sacrifices are made (or proposed) for the sake of upholding conventional morality.
3. *Post-conventional* – existing rules and laws are transcended in favour of personally derived moral principles, which involve universal

moral principles such as individual rights, respect for life, justice and equality. There is no single moral reality, and there is recognition that existing conventions may fail to serve universal principles. At this level, multiple possibilities are seen. For example: 'Although stealing is illegal, in this case he would try to save his wife's life, or indeed the life of anyone, and hope that others would do the same for him'.

Kohlberg's stage model of moral thought has been criticized, for example on the grounds that it is culturally limited, and methodologically and conceptually problematic (Kurtines, 1986; Batson et al., 1993). Emler et al. (1998) have shown partial support for the idea that particular types of moral judgment are the result of ideological identity, rather than intellectual or moral 'maturity'. Nevertheless it remains an important contribution to the understanding of moral thinking, and an important foundation of Fowler's work.

Fowler

Table 4.5 shows Fowler's systematization of the parallels between stages of development in different theories.

The meanings of some of the terms in the table might be a little hard to envisage. The box on p.72 may help to translate Fowler's rather abstract summary into the terms of everyday experience. It shows part of a faith scale, based on the work of Fowler, developed by Barnes et al. (1989). The scale is a useful summary of the ideas that are typical of the middle four of Fowler's six stages in faith development, which are the most common among adults. Fowler used the term faith in a broad sense, 'philosophy of life', rather as Allport (1950) did. Explicit religious affiliation and doctrinal acceptance is not necessary, in Fowler's view, to the development of mature faith. If you wish to assess yourself, select which of each pair of statements reflects your views more accurately – but to get a fair score you should cover up the figures in brackets on the left-hand side of the page until you have completed all your choices. When you have finished making your choices, you can give a score to each of your choices, which will be the number in brackets next to it. Your final score can be worked out by adding the six scores together and dividing by 6. You should get a number, somewhere between 2 and 5. A score like 4.23, for instance, would suggest that you have a rather mature level of faith (in Fowler's scheme). The scale was developed to be relevant to Roman Catholics, and if you are a Christian of a different denomination, or an adherent of a non-

Table 4.5 Fowler's stages in the development of faith, and parallels with other cognitive-developmental theories (adapted from Fowler, 1981)

Stage	Aspect				
	Form of logic (Piaget)	Moral judgement (Kohlberg)	Bounds of social awareness	Form of world coherence	Symbolic function
I	Pre-operational	Punishment - reward	Family, primal others	Episodic	Magical – numinous one-dimensional.
II	Concrete operational	Instrumental hedonism	'Those like us'	Narrative - dramatic	Literal
III	Early formal operations	Interpersonal expectation and concordance	Consensus of valued groups	Felt meanings symbolically mediated	Evocative power in symbol
IV	Formal operations (dichotomizing)	Social perspective	Ideologically compatible communities	Explicit system	Symbols separated from symbolized
V	Formal operations (dialectical)	Principled	Extends beyond class norms and interests	Multi-systemic symbolic mediation	Postcritical rejoining of irreducible power and ideational meaning
VI	Formal operations (synthetic)	Loyalty to being	Experienced judgement, not egoistic	Unitive actuality felt	Evocative power of symbols

Christian religion, remember the scale was not meant to apply to you and your score may not mean much.

---◆---

A SHORTENED FORM OF A SCALE FOR ASSESSING LEVEL OF RELIGIOUS FAITH OF ROMAN CATHOLICS, BASED ON FOWLER

(2) 1a. Those who do what God wants are given special rewards.

(3) 1b. God grants comfort and strength to those who are loyal and faithful.

(2) 2a. God can do what God wants without any particular reason.

(4) 2b. It is important to try and make sense out of how God acts and why.

(2) 3a. A good way to relate to God is to do what God wants, so that God will help you in return.

(5) 3b. It is best to think of God as utterly and freely giving.

(3) 4a. It is important to follow the leaders to whom God has entrusted his church.

(4) 4b. Religious leaders must respect the need for reasonableness, consistency, and coherence in their interpretation of doctrines.

(3) 5a. It is often hard to understand why people are disloyal to their family and religion.

(5) 5b. People have to make their own best choices about religion, even if it means following new ways.

(4) 6a. God's revealed truth is meant for all people everywhere.

(5) 6b. No set of religious beliefs is the whole and final truth for everyone.

Adapted from Barnes *et al.*, 1989

---◆---

To give more of the flavour of religious thinking at different stages, here are two illustrations from Fowler's interviews:

Stage 1 (Freddy) (after offering some anthropomorphic images of God): 'He spreads all around the world in one day ... 'cause he's smart (that's how he knows when someone does something bad). He can do things that are good, not bad. God never told a lie in his life'.

Stage 5 (Miss T) 'I would say that one of the things that has come to me in the last few days is that this cosmic flow, which is God, call it what you will ... has come to me more deeply'.

More recent discussions of Fowler's work and its developments and implications appear in Fowler *et al.* (1991).

Spero

A further account of faith development which draws on Fowler's work, and which uses clinical case material, is Spero's (1992). This is a valuable account, because (following Meissner, 1984) it gives a fuller picture of the kinds of beliefs about God characteristic of the different stages of faith, and it also helps us to understand how different beliefs about God might go along with different kinds of mental health and ill-health. Spero has added a psychoanalytic perspective to an approach that is otherwise like Fowler's in many respects. He shows how religious concepts can change over a relatively short time-span, in the course of psychological counselling (see box).

---◆---

Spero (1992) describes the case of a medical student who suffered from obsessive-compulsive neurosis, with hypochondriasis and somatization:
'He was a prematurely sardonic judge of human inconsistency and hypocrisy. He lambasted those who differed from him religiously. As a youngster he had tried to escape the surveillance of the strict God of his teachers.
In the course of therapy, he developed a sense of mystery, respect for others, a new experience of himself as a physician, as a person in relation to God, who he no longer perceived as pillorying or ridiculing him.'

---◆---

In this outline of different approaches to understanding the development of religious faith, the most important single theme to emerge is the interconnection of religious faith to other aspects of the individual's life and personal development. Faith, it seems, is borne from the union of abstract ideas conveyed in words, with life experiences. Particularly interesting are the beliefs that may be associated with experiences that are specifically religious or mystical. These experiences and their associated ideas and feelings are discussed in the next chapter.

Is faith a culturally-limited concept? This is of course partly a theological question, which could be answered by a study of authoritative religious texts and other sources from different religions around the world, beyond the scope of this book. In London-based research (Cinnirella and Loewenthal, 1999; Loewenthal and Cinnirella, 1999a), it appeared that members of different religious groups hold very similar ideas about the role of religious faith and trust, in coping with serious stress, and otherwise. Among those interviewed were immigrants from

South Asia, both Muslim and Hindu, Afro-Caribbeans and Jews (mostly the children of immigrants), as well as native British Christians.

◆

THE ROLE OF RELIGION IN COPING WITH STRESS AND DEPRESSION

These quotations are from a series of interviews with women talking about the role of religious faith, trust, prayer and other religious means which might be used in coping with life stress and depression.

'It's true that people who have a blind faith in God will not get depressed, but if they do they will come out of it very quickly because they believe that whatever is happening is happening for their good and they accept this thing from their heart. When our faith is weak, we go deeper and deeper into depression.' (Muslim woman)

"If you believe in God, praying would help because you have faith in something, but not everyone believes in God, so not everyone will be able to benefit from praying.' (Hindu woman)

"People can find faith in their lowest moments, can't they?' (Hindu woman)

'A holy person might be able to say, look, God will help you through this, have faith. But if a person did not believe in God initially they probably wouldn't even think of going to a holy person. Belief is stronger (among Hindus in Britain) in the older generation.' (Hindu woman)

'I suspect yes (belief in God would help a person) ... personally I don't have a deep core that believes in something else ... so it's not helped me, but I think for some people it could well be a lifeline.' (White British Christian woman)

'I think it does help (to trust that whatever God does is for the best). I think in a depressed state, this I can cope with ... I can say ... all right God if this is your idea of a joke that's fine, I'll go along with it ... but depression can in a sense squash trust.' (Jewish woman)

'I think that's the hardest, to trust that whatever happens is for the best, to have faith ... you've got to be quite fit and well to do that.' (White British Christian woman)

'If one bad thing after another keeps happening ... believing that it's all for the best can help people get through this, can help them survive, can help them lift spirits ... just keep going. It can be a support, knowing that God is there, looking after you ... that it's all part of his divine plan, can help you survive.' (Afro-Caribbean Christian woman)

Quoted in Cinnirella and Loewenthal, 1999; Loewenthal and Cinnirella, 1999a

◆

In spite of their personal differences in level of religious faith, and in cultural background and religious tradition, all these women subscribed to the view that religious faith and trust can help its fortunate possessor in times of stress, and may help to relieve depression. The concept of religious faith was familiar to all in spite of wide variations in religiosity and religious tradition.

SUMMARY

This chapter first looked at some quantitative studies of religious belief, and then turned to studies of the quality of religious belief, and changes over the life-span. Faith development was also examined. A number of developmental studies and models were considered, including those of Piaget, Goldman, Thun, Erikson, Kohlberg and Fowler.

5 RELIGIOUS FEELINGS

What do you understand by the term 'religious feelings'? These feelings might be pleasant, and would most likely include awe, love, mysticism, and trust. There might be negative feelings, fear or anger for example. Or there might be a blank – often labelled as disbelief. In this chapter we will first look at Freud's and other psychoanalytic hypotheses about the origins of religious feelings – both pleasant and unpleasant. Then we will explore some psychological perspectives on some of the positive feelings that are associated with religion, including those associated with various religious experiences, before turning to unpleasant feelings and disbelief.

EARLY ORIGINS OF RELIGIOUS FEELINGS

Freud

Freud was not the only early twentieth-century writer to discuss the psychological origins of religious feelings, but he is probably the best remembered, and at the time he wrote, he was probably the most notorious. Freud had developed psychoanalysis, a method of treating psychological illness by means of talking. His views on the origins of religion were notorious for three reasons:

1. they appeared at the time to 'explain away' religion;
2. they were often derogatory;
3. he was generally notorious because he had made a number of unacceptable suggestions about the existence of child sexual abuse, and about sexual feelings among young children.

Freud was born into a somewhat assimilated Jewish family, who moved to Vienna when Freud was a young child. Freud remained proud of his Jewish identity, maintained some traditional Jewish practice and was active in Viennese Jewish life. He experienced professional frustration, failing to gain academic security or promotion, probably because of anti-Semitism (Jones, 1953). Until about the age of forty, he carried out academic research, mainly in neurophysiology. Although his work in this field is still well thought of, he was not awarded any significant promotion, perhaps as suggested because of anti-Semitism. He then turned to private medical practice, specializing in the treatment of nervous disorders, and developed the famous 'talking cure' – psychoanalysis. He lived almost all the rest of his life in Vienna until he fled the Nazis as a very old man. He died in London. (Jones, 1953, 1955, 1957). He published prolifically on psychoanalysis from the last decade of the nineteenth century onwards, over a period of nearly fifty years. He published several books on religion: *The Future of an Illusion* (1927), *Totem and Taboo* (1928), *Civilisation and its Discontents* (1930) and *Moses and Monotheism* (1939). Freud's most important theories about religion were based on his view of psychological development in young children. Freud suggested that the young child experienced strong feelings towards their opposite-sex parent, including a wish to possess and control. At the same time the child feared that the same-sex parent would punish the child for these wishes. Freud suggested that the young child tried to resolve this dilemma by *identifying* with the same-sex parent, and *internalizing* a parent-image. This resolves the dilemma by gaining vicarious possession of the opposite-sex parent, while pleasing both parents: 's/he is just like his mum/dad'. The image of God is based on the image of the father, in Freud's view.

This account of Freud's suggestions is simplified; there are a number of difficulties and inconsistencies in Freud's suggestions, and they differed somewhat for boys and for girls. But few would seriously dispute the occurrence of something like internalization and identification.

One of the best-known features of Freud's theories of religion is that religion is a form of neurosis. In Freud's view religion is a universal collective neurosis, which saves the person the task of forming their own private neurosis. Freud (1905) suggested that religious ritual has many of the features of obsessive–compulsive disorder. Describing a woman with a compulsion to wash her hands and to scour out the basin, Freud compared this to religious ritual:

- The person feels guilty if the action is not carried out. Performing the action brings relief, but this is temporary. There is a further build-up of anxiety, relieved again by carrying out the ritual. A self-perpetuating cycle is set up.
- The person does not normally perceive the symbolic significance of their actions.
- However religious and private neurotic rituals differ in that the former are publicly taught and widely practised.

Freud's best known theory about religion is probably that the image of God is based on that of the father, and the origins of religion are the internalization of the father-figure. Provocatively, Freud declared that although the Bible states that God created man in his image, Freud states that man creates God in his image. Numerous tests of Freud's idea have been carried out, that the God image and the father-image are similar, and that people's feelings about God will be similar to their feelings about their father. The box below shows how this might be (and has been) done.

◆

EXAMPLES OF QUESTIONS COMPARING THE GOD IMAGE WITH THE FATHER-IMAGE

1. On each of the lines below, place an X to show how you see God:

KIND _____ CRUEL
BAD _____ GOOD
FAIR _____ UNFAIR
[etc.]

2. On each of the lines below, place an X to show how you see your father:

KIND _____ CRUEL
BAD _____ GOOD
FAIR _____ UNFAIR
[etc.]

3. On each of the lines below, place an X to show how you see your mother:

KIND _____ CRUEL
BAD _____ GOOD
FAIR _____ UNFAIR
[etc.]

◆

A large number of studies have shown that there is little noteworthy support for Freud's hypothesis in its original form. People might see a resemblance between God and their father, but they are likely to see an equally strong or stronger resemblance between God and their mother. It may depend on who is the preferred parent, the amount and type of religious education, cultural–religious tradition and other factors. (Argyle and Beit-Hallahmi, 1974; Vergote and Tamayo, 1980; Loewenthal, 1995).

There are many problems with Freud's theories of religion. For instance, if, as Freud suggested, girls identify with their mothers, then the image of God might be expected to be more like that of the mother among girls. There is little evidence of this kind of gender difference. However, it is unwise to dismiss the important idea that early family relations might have an important impact upon religious feelings and ideas. This fundamental idea is a legacy from Freud, and we turn to examine some variants.

Object-relations theory

Object-relations theory is a development from the work of Melanie Klein (1932, 1975). Klein had a Freudian psycho-analytic training, fled Nazi persecution in Austria, and worked in London chiefly as a child analyst. Her views had a major influence on the development of psychoanalysis in Britain, and object-relations theory owes its origins to her. She in turn owes her fundamental thinking to Freud, in spite of sharp divergences.

An important difference between Klein and Freud is their emphasis on different periods in child development. Freud's infant is a somewhat opaque creature, who feeds and bites and defecates. This view of the infant is most associated with fathers, which is of course what Freud was. It was slightly older children (two- to five year olds) – those of an age he, as a father, perhaps had more to do with – who were the main source of interest and inspiration to Freud in formulating his theories of character development, the origins of the neuroses, and the origins of religion. Klein, as a mother, would have spent hundreds of hours holding, nursing, soothing, dealing with and being with her young infant children, and it was the feelings of children of this early age that resonated most strongly with her. For Klein, the young infant is (psychologically) in the paranoid-schizoid position. The infant's world is one of part-objects, in which good and bad, love and hate, care and indifference, gentleness and harshness cannot co-exist in one object. In Klein's extraordinary terminology, the infant's attention is focused on the breast, and the loving-mother experience is encapsulated in the part-object, the good breast. Conversely the rejecting-mother experience is encapsulated in the bad breast. The child splits good and bad part-objects, and the bad part-objects become externalized (projected) and persecutory. Hence the term paranoid-schizoid. The splitting and projecting which are characteristic of the early infantile paranoid-schizoid position can remain enduring characteristics of our thinking. The bogies of nightmares, the demons and enemies that persecute, and all those nasty people that we know, that are nothing like our own nice selves – these are all the result of splitting and projection. It is an unusual adult that does not entertain or even foster hatred, envy, greed or jealousy, all emotions that arise from and feed upon splitting and projection.

Klein suggested that at a later stage in development, the child is able to fuse part-objects, to feel that one and the same object is able to be both good and bad. The child can contain both good and bad in one object – without splitting and projection. The growth of the appreciation of the other, and sensitivity to their pain, is a direct result of the ability to fuse part-objects into whole objects. Instead of being other, dangerous, wicked, to be damaged and destroyed, the other becomes a feeling being. Now, according to Klein, the capacity for regret and guilt appears, regret and guilt over damage caused by destructive and damaging behaviour. This sorrow leads to the wish to make reparation, to heal and to restore. In Klein's terminology, the capacity for sympathy, for regret and the wish to repair, are all features of the depressive position.

This outline of the shift from the paranoid-schizoid to the depressive position indicates the central core of Kleinian theory. It has been developed by contemporary object-relations theorists, several of whom are interested in the applications of object-relations theory to the understanding of religion.

It is quite possible to appreciate, for instance, how a schizoid-paranoid style of religiosity could involve a splitting of the world into good and bad part-objects – perhaps a good self, good fellow-members of ones religious group, and a bad outside world, for example. In the depressive position, a more humane, tolerant and positive style of religiosity would be expected. A very similar distinction has been made by psychological theorists who would not claim any relationship with object-relations theory – Allport (1950) for example (see chapter 6), Jung (1958), or Fromm (1950).

Finn and Gartner's anthology (1992) includes a range of clinical applications of object-relations theory and religion. Rizzuto for example (1974, 1979, 1992) suggested that the image of God is formed from elements which originated in early object representations and interactions. Although this image has some potential for change, it is the early object relations that are the most important and lasting elements of the internalized image of God. Rizzuto described four broad types of relationship with God:

1) 'I have a God.'
2) 'I might have a God.'
3) 'I do not have a God.'
4) 'I have a God but I wish I did not.'

Note that the second and third types, doubt and disbelief, qualify as relationships with God.

◆

Mr Miller says he has no religion, does not pray, and is unsure of the existence of God. He says he has not formulated any specific ideas about God because the need to do so has not come up. Mr Miller had been a restless, crying baby, and his mother found it difficult to look after him, both as a baby and as a child. Discipline was left to his father, a hard-working and conscientious man. Although as a young child, he had an exceptional memory, he suffered from reading problems, and Mr Miller did not do particularly well in school or college, much to his father's disappointment. After some psychological help, he did obtain a job. Here are some pairs of statements made by Mr Miller about his father and about God:

Father	God
I was never close to my father.	I have never experienced closeness to God.
I don't talk to my father.	I do not formally pray.
I do not ask anything from my father.	If I am in distress I do not resort to God because I have no belief in God.
My father always insisted I (make) the best use of my abilities.	If there is a God, then I have dissatisfied him, because I have not made the best use of my abilities.

(Described in Rizzuto, 1974)

◆

Another theorist who believes that object-relations theory is important for understanding religious ideas and feelings, is Spero (1992) whose views were outlined in chapter 4 (page 73).

On the whole, the clinical implications of the object-relations theory view of religious feelings have been explored and expounded quite thoroughly. However, systematic empirical investigations have not been done.

Attachment theory

Bowlby (1969, 1973, 1980) has developed a view on the social and emotional world of early infancy which owes something to the observations of ethologists, studying the attachment of infant animals and birds to adults of the same (or sometimes other) species. The main applications of Bowlby's attachment theory have been clinical and psychotherapeutic (Bartholomew, 1997; Birtchnell, 1997; Harris, 1997). Kirkpatrick (1992, 1997) has developed an application of Bowlby's attachment theory to religion, and this application of attachment theory has been systematically investigated with some promising results. When applied to the psychology of religion, the theory is rather startling. Although the ideas are fundamentally quite simple, they give a different picture of the origins of religious feelings to that based on Freudian theory. And the empirical support, so far at least, seems more convincing.

Kirkpatrick's attachment-theory view of religion is based on Bowlby's distinction between three broad patterns of attachment between infants and their adult caretakers (usually mothers). The three patterns are *secure, anxious/avoidant*, and *mixed* (i.e. both secure and anxious/avoidant). Somewhat paradoxically (at least to those who have never had dealings with a clingy baby) the securely-attached infant feels more free to leave the mother and to explore, than does the infant with anxious/avoidant and mixed attachment styles. The box below shows part of a self-report measure of attachment style, designed for adults. This measure separates anxious and avoidant styles into two distinct styles, even though Bowlby observed that in infancy both types of behaviour were often present in one relationship.

ADULT ATTACHMENT SCALE (PART ONLY)

1. I am comfortable depending on others. (Secure)
2. I find others are reluctant to get as close as I would like. (Anxious)
3. I am somewhat uncomfortable being close to others. (Avoidant)
4. I find it relatively easy to get close to others. (Secure)
5. I want to merge completely with another person. (Anxious)
6. I find it difficult to trust others completely. (Avoidant)

(Collins and Read, 1990)

Kirkpatrick and Shaver (1990) assessed recalled attachment styles of college students with their mothers, when they were young children. Those who had reported a 'cold', anxious/avoidant relationship with their mothers were more likely to have undergone a *sudden* religious conversion. Their relationship with God was reported to be more close and personal, than for those whose relationships with their mothers were described as warm and secure. These latter subjects showed a more laid-back type of religiosity (or lack of religiosity), usually following in their mothers' footsteps, without undergoing any obvious crises.

There are several interesting differences between the Freudian and object-relations approaches to religion, compared to the attachment-theory based approach. The Freudian and object-relations approach tends to emphasize the relationship with the father, while attachment theory emphasizes the relationship with the primary caretaker (usually the mother). Freudian approaches deal with elaborate specifications of the quality of early relationships, while attachment theory offers a devastatingly simple typology – secure versus anxious/avoidant. Freudian and object-relations theories of religion tend to focus on the influence of early relationships on the image of God (and hence the quality of the relationship between the individual and God). Attachment theory offers quite elaborate predictions about religious biographies, as well as about the quality and intensity of individual relationships with God. Both kinds of theory have a great deal to offer for the understanding of the origins of religious feelings.

Recent evaluations

In this section on the early origins of religious feelings we turn to two recent studies, one of children and one of psychologists of religion.

An enduring question is to do with the importance and fundamental nature of early experiences. Do they have a special status? Do they, for example, set up a framework into which later experience has to be fitted? To what extent are early experiences determined by 'innate' characteristics of the child which may continue to influence behaviour and hence social experience? Or can the effects of early experiences be overlaid, and if so under what circumstances? These questions continue to be debated, both in the context of the psychology of religion and elsewhere.

DICKIE ET AL.

The first study to be considered (Dickie et al. 1997). looks at the question of early relationships, and how they affect feelings about God, and how and when these feelings change. Dickie et al. looked at the feelings of children aged four to eleven years, from a range of different cultural backgrounds, towards both parents and towards God. They considered a number of hypotheses derived from attachment theory and several other (developmental) theories, and among their findings were the following:

- Perception of God resembled perception of *both* parents;
- God was seen as more nurturant by those children whose *father* was more nurturant;
- God was seen as more powerful by those whose *mother* was seen as more powerful (thus *father's* nurturance and *mother's* power predict, respectively, God's nurturance and power);
- There were a number of differences between boys and girls, both in the way they saw their parents and in the way they saw God. For example, girls' images of God were more related to parent's perceived attributes and discipline styles than were boys. The younger girls rated both God and their father as significantly less powerful than did the boys. Not all of these effects were in accordance with hypotheses from developmental theory;
- Older children saw God as more nurturing and more powerful than did younger children.

Dickie et al. thought this indicated support for attachment theory: God did appear to become the 'perfect substitute attachment figure'.

The study by Dickie *et al.* is in many ways typical of modern empirical work involving multivariate analysis, and it has yielded a wealth of findings interesting to the psychologist of religion, and including support for the currently popular attachment theory approach.

CAPPS' 'MEN, RELIGION AND MELANCHOLY'

A different contemporary approach to understanding the impact of early relationships on religious feelings is advanced by Donald Capps. Capps' source materials are the writings and biographical materials relating to the lives of four very famous and influential psychologists of religion: William James, Rudolf Otto, Carl Jung and Erik Erikson. Capps' book is particularly interesting because he has developed a thesis from Freud's writings about the origins of religion that is quite different from two better-known Freudian hypotheses. The two well-known theses are that God is a father-figure, and that religion is a universal (obsessional) neurosis, both of which stem from Freud's description of the so-called Oedipal situation in which the young boy identifies with his father. Instead, Capps draws on Freud's *Mourning and Melancholia* (1963), and *The Uncanny* (1958). Drawing on these, Capps' hypothesis is that men may fall into melancholia as a result of the loss of the close, carefree loving relationship experienced with the mother. Melancholy is translated into religious feelings. By careful (though speculative) analysis of biographical material, Capps suggests that each of the subjects of his analysis had an unusual and idiosyncratic definition or view of religion, that was related to his relationship with his mother (see Table 5.1, p. 86).

Table 5.1 oversimplifies Capps' argument, but suggests enough to show how – without overlooking the importance of the father – it can be argued that the relationship with the mother has an important effect on religious feelings. Of course, Capps' subjects were very distinguished scholars, with a professional interest in religion and in its psychological aspects. It therefore remains to be seen how far Capps' suggestions might apply to other men, and to women.

POSITIVE FEELINGS

Mystical feelings

Mystical feelings are sometimes thought of as the most typically *religious* of religious feelings, and have been extensively documented in scholarly works on religious mystical traditions (e.g. Huxley, 1954; Stace, 1960).

LIVERPOOL
JOHN MOORES UNIVERSITY
AVRIL ROBARTS LRC
TITHEBARN STREET
LIVERPOOL L2 2ER

Table 5.1   *Four famous views of religion, and important features of the mother-son relationship* (based on Capps 1997)

Author	Definition	Relationship with mother
James (1902)	The feelings of individual men in their solitude.	James saw his mother as oblivious to his feelings, and he did not wish to disturb that oblivion.
Otto (1958)	The numinous, involving a 'thrill of fear'.	Otto's mother became inaccessible, preoccupied with many other children. Otto may have (deliberately) provoked her chastisement.
Jung (1969)	After searching in vain everywhere God rises 'like a little sun in his own heart'.	Jung's mother disappeared (into hospital) when he was young, and he afterwards regarded women as unreliable.
Erikson (1958)	Coming to terms with own self-hatred.	Erikson's mother welcomed an intruder (step-father) into the mother-son idyllic relationship (causing Erikson's own self-hatred).

There is quite a wide range of different mystical feelings, and some may not be considered specifically religious (Hay, 1994).

Here is an example, quoted by Wulff (1997) from Masters and Houston's (1973) study:

> 'The whole experience was so positive and profound that I was in a state of total awe and wonder ... I feel myself to be boundlessly happy and at complete acceptance and peace with myself ... I feel myself to be in an active connection with the harmony and unity of nature and of the cosmos'.

Psychologists and others have been interested in these kinds of states for many years. In fact the earliest classic work on the psychology of religion, William James' *The Varieties of Religious Experience* (1902) was largely devoted to their analysis and understanding. Other notable contributions include the philosopher Stace's (1960) *Mysticism and Philosophy*, which defined the introvertive mystical experience, and the work of Hood (1975), Hardy (1975) and Hay (1987).

Stace distinguished several sorts of mystical experience, and his definition of the introvertive mystical experience has been used to help understand the circumstances in which such experiences are more likely. Pahnke (1966) adapted Stace's criteria as follows:

1. The experience of *unity* or oneness, perceived either outwardly in the external world, or inwardly, in a state of pure awareness that is free of all distinctions, including the sense of being a separate self.
2. *Transcendence of time and space*, into 'eternity' and 'infinity'.
3. *A deeply felt positive mood*, of utter joy, blessedness and peace.
4. The *sense of sacredness*, prompting a response of awe and wonder.
5. A conviction of *objectivity and reality*, an intuitively sensed knowledge or illumination of one's finite self as well as of ultimate reality.
6. A quality of *paradoxicality* or logical inconsistency, as in the mystical assertion that the empty unity is at the same time full and complete.
7. *Alleged ineffability* or indescribableness, in spite of the mystic's continuing efforts to relate what they have experienced.
8. *Transiency*, a shortness of duration that contrasts with the ongoingness of ordinary experience.
9. *Persistent positive changes in attitude and behaviour*, including increased integration of personality, more sensitivity and love toward others, a new, richer appreciation of life and its meaning, and a deeper sense of the value of mystical experience.

Pahnke used these criteria to examine the circumstances under which a drug (psilocybin) might foster the occurrence of mystical experiences as defined above. The participants in Pahnke's research took part in a Good Friday service, and Pahnke's findings suggest that the context of religious preparation is important for mystical experience to occur.

Ralph Hood (1975) has investigated the circumstances and personality correlates of mystical experiences among North Americans. Hood has also used Stace-type criteria for defining mystical experience, and he has produced a measure in which people can indicate the extent to which they have had, for example, 'an experience which was both timeless and spaceless'.

Sir Alister Hardy, a British zoologist, founded the Religious Experience Research Unit (now known as the Alister Hardy Research Centre, the AHRC) in Oxford. Hardy (1965, 1966, 1975) suggested that humans had a natural capacity for religious experience, and the role of the AHRC was to investigate these experiences. Thousands of reports were collected. Initially, Hardy (1979) asked: 'Have you ever been aware of or influenced by a presence or a power, whether you call it God or not, which is different from your everyday self?'

This question is not so closely based on Stace's criteria as were Pahnke's and Hood's, but Hay (1994) noted that questions about mystical experience may be worded very differently and still produce very similar answers. Hay headed the AHRC for several years, and reported that between 1970 and 1987, in national surveys in Britain, Australia and the USA, between twenty and forty eight per cent of those surveyed said that they had had at least one mystical experience. Typically about one-third of those surveyed reported mystical experience. Hay believes that Hardy's hypothesis about the biology of God is supported, namely that religious experience is biologically based. Hay believes that this is a more plausible explanation for religious experience than, say, Freud's hypothesis that religion is a form of neurosis. The AHRC researchers have found that religious experience is predominantly pleasant, although one of the eight types of experience they identified included awareness of an evil presence.

Beardsworth (1977), Hardy (1979) and Hay (1987) identified eight kinds of religious experience on the basis of people's reports. In order of frequency these were:

- a patterning of events in a person's life that convince him or her that in some strange way they were meant to happen;
- an awareness of the presence of God;
- an awareness of receiving help in answer to prayer;
- an awareness of being looked after or guided by a presence not called God;
- an awareness of being in the presence of someone who has died;
- an awareness of a sacred presence in nature;
- an awareness of an evil presence;
- experiencing in an extraordinary way that all things are 'One'.

In spite of variations in how religious and mystical experience is defined, there does seem to be some agreement that these experiences are *wide-*

spread and *pleasant*. Of the many other features identified, Hay (1994) has clearly signalled what is crucial: '... the awareness of a sacred or divine presence is experienced paradoxically as 'sensory' yet unaccompanied by any of the normal sensory inputs'.

Hay says that it might seem strange that an apprehension of something with a clear cognitive component is possible in the absence of sensory input. Nevertheless, he suggests that there are parallel cases of recognition 'at an affective level, detected by measures of emotional response'.

Religious visons

Religious visions are different to pure introvertive mystical experiences. A normal healthy person can experience visions, either when asleep, in dreams, or when falling asleep, in hypnagogic imagery. A vision is an experience resembling that of actually seeing something, but there is normally an awareness that what is seen is not physically present in the person's surroundings. Young children are not aware that the dream or hypnagogic image is not physically present in the environment. Few parents have escaped having to comfort a terrified pre-schooler, frightened by nightmares that seem to be 'real'; whereas a nine-year-old can say: 'If a horrible monster comes along in a dream, I tell it to go away and get lost, otherwise – I'll wake up (and then it will be finished!).' Schizophrenia has been described as a waking dream, from which the sufferer is unable to awaken. This is now thought to be due to structural anatomical features of the pathways controlling attention (e.g. Cohen *et al.*, 1998). Visions and hallucinations can be induced by drugs, or by electrical stimulation of the brain (Penfield and Perot, 1963). Some visions may be symptoms of psychosis. But religious visions, although felt to be 'real', are clearly recognized by the visionary as visions of an alternative reality, not of the mundane physical worlds. Lipsedge (1996) discusses Kroll and Bachrach's (1982) search of historical records of 134 religious visionary experiences from the lives of saints, church and other records, in England and France, between the years 600 and 1300. All descriptions of visions, voices and dreams judged as *a visio* were examined. About half occurred in dreams or while falling asleep. About half the remainder were in the context of an organic confusional state, such as fever or starvation. Of the remaining quarter, about half occurred under stress, such as battle, and the rest occurred under everyday circumstances, such as the 'vision of the mother of Mercy seen and heard while at prayer by the monk Herbert'. Only a tiny proportion occurred during episodes of mental illness. This suggests, as with Pahnke's conclusions about mystical experience, that physical and psychological conditions might precipitate religious experiences, but a religious context is needed to give the experiences their uniquely religious character.

Lipsedge goes on to say that although visions are unlikely to be a definitive sign of madness, they may be taken as such. It might have been genuinely hard to tell whether Josephina, described in the box below, was truly mad, or merely a political nuisance. One could suspect the latter.

◆

Josephina was a Zulu and a prophetess. Her African separatist speeches attracted large audiences at meetings of the South African Native Congress. In 1932, the police reported that Josephina had said that the word of the Lord had come to her in a vision at night. She had seen a hand writing on the wall in indelible pencil that she should go to the South African people and warn them that it would be dark for twelve days, and that locusts with the faces of men would come in the winter. She said that the time had come for the Europeans, Indians and Chinese to leave South Africa and go back to the lands from which they came.

(Lipsedge, 1996)

◆

What of the report that religious visions and other religious experiences are more likely among those who suffer from epilepsy? Fenwick (1996) believes that the evidence is equivocal. In a British study based on the Maudsley Hospital, Sensky and Fenwick (1982) found that those with temporal lobe epilepsy were no more inclined to religion than those with generalized epilepsy, or normal controls. More crucially, epileptics reported no more – and sometimes less – experience of mystical and psychic states than normal controls (see Table 5.2).

Near-death and out-of-body experiences

These fascinating experiences are often given a religious interpretation, in the sense that the person may interpret their experience as one in which their soul (or some non-corporeal aspect of the self) leaves the

Table 5.2   Reported religiosity and mystical experience among those suffering from temporal lobe epilepsy and generalized epilepsy, compared with general population controls (Fenwick, 1996; Hay and Morisy, 1978)

	Temporal lobe epilepsy (%)	Generalized epilepsy (%)	General population (%)
Regard self as religious	56	72	57
Sudden gain of faith	40	62	42
In touch with the universe	12	33	19

body, and is aware both of the events surrounding the body, and of other features which may be interpreted as other-worldly. The normative report includes the following features (Moody, 1985):

- The experience is not deliberately sought after or engaged in. It follows severe illness, surgery, or injury.
- The person has been at the point of death, or even reported as clinically dead.
- The experience is of being out of the body and aware of what is happening in the surroundings. For example, the person may hear and remember what people around the body are saying, and can report this accurately afterwards.
- Subsequently there may be an experience of being drawn towards 'light'.
- There may be experiences of being in touch with people who they knew, but who have previously died.
- Feelings of peace are common, and feelings of longing to merge with the light are sometimes reported.
- Some people have said they (or their soul) were informed that their mission in life is not yet completed and they must return to their body.
- Many people report a deep and positive effect on inner, psychological and/or spiritual life.

As with other forms of religious experience, there has been some speculation about the physiological conditions under which such near-death experiences (NDEs) and out-of-body experiences are likely (Fenwick, 1987; Blackmore, 1993). Fenwick, for example, suggested that these experiences may be more likely in people with a history of epilepsy.

◆

Rachel Noam gives an account of a specific near-death experience (NDE). She was walking down a city street when the events happened. The details she describes are characteristic of an NDE, though at the time she had never heard of the phenomenon. She thought her experience was unusual, and did not at first disclose it to anyone except very close confidants, for fear that she should be considered deranged.

She had been struck on the head by a huge beam that had fallen from the top of a high building under construction. She was knocked flat and lost consciousness. She suddenly felt she was outside her body, floating upward about twelve to fifteen feet above the sidewalk, watching the scene below. She did not know how she got there. Bystanders examined her body, and she could hear them calling for help and demanding to speak to the building contractor who was responsible for the fallen beam. She could hear the contractor refusing to come. She was puzzled as to how she could see and hear, without eyes and ears, or indeed a body of any kind. 'Obviously I existed, I was real, I was conscious, but not inside my frame.' She felt free of pain, relaxed, and remained conscious of her inert body below.

Then she became aware of a gradual change. 'The events in the street began to fade away into darkness, and through this darkness, I perceived a glimmer of brightness. As the radiance came closer it grew in intensity, becoming a glorious powerful light, radiating an abundant flow of exalted spirituality. In harmony with this flow of illumination, the events in my life began to pass before my eyes. The images were three-dimensional, and I saw myself taking part in them. My entire life flashed by, from the day I was born until the very moment I fell to the ground ... The entire experience filled me with an indescribable sense of exalted happiness. Once again, I saw the blinding luminescence, glowing in a soft velvety white, as if an infinite number of brightly flashing magic sparks were uniting in a burst of spectacular brilliance ... The magnificent stream of light was accompanied by a flow of sublime love, a kind of love I had never before experienced ... I felt incapable of remaining an independent entity; I simply melted away. I was too small to withstand the flow of goodness streaming toward me and into me. I tried to defend myself, to close my eyes, but I had no eyes to close! ... my "self" dissolved into nothingness ... I felt a strong pull to become part of this wonderful eternal flow... "I am drawn to following my inclination," I said, but I ask to be returned to my body. I ask to be given another opportunity in this world.'

(Noam, 1992)

◆

The experience of Rachel Noam (see box) shows most of the features common to NDEs: out-of-body experience, hearing, seeing and recalling conversations and behaviour of people around one's body, an experience of a great light, a fast replay of life experiences, a sense of love. Other NDE reports include an experience like passing through a tunnel before encountering the light, and meeting people who have previously died (or their souls). Many NDEs include an experience in which the person becomes aware that they are to return to their bodies since their mission in life is unfinished. Many people report that they have been affected in a positive way by their experiences, feeling a stronger awareness of the spiritual side of their nature, a stronger belief in non-material existence, and a stronger sense of purpose in life.

Spiritual Well-Being

Positive religious feelings are not confined to isolated experiences, which may only be of a brief duration. Religious feelings may be quite stable. This is the claim made by Ellison (Paloutzian and Ellison, 1982; Ellison, 1983; Bufford, Paloutzian and Ellison, 1991). Ellison developed a measure, the Spiritual Well-Being Scale (SWB) (see box) which involves two factors, Religious Well-Being (RWB) and Existential Well-Being (EWB). Scores on this test tend to be stable, at least over the periods of time intervals used (up to ten weeks).

◆

THE SPIRITUAL WELL-BEING SCALE

Religious Well-Being Items

*I don't find much satisfaction in private prayer with God.
I believe God loves me and cares about me.
*I believe that God is impersonal and not interested in my daily situations.
I have a personally meaningful relationship with God.
*I don't get much personal strength and support from my God.
I believe that God is concerned about my problems.
*I don't have a personally satisfying relationship with God.
My relationship with God helps me not to feel lonely.
I feel most fulfilled when I'm in close communion with God.
My relationship with God contributes to my sense of well-being.

Existential Well-Being Items

*I don't know who I am, where I came from, or where I'm going.
I feel that life is a positive experience.
*I feel unsettled about my future.
I feel very fulfilled and satisfied with life.
I feel a sense of well-being about the direction my life is headed in.
*I don't enjoy much about life.
I feel good about my future.
*I feel that life is full of conflict and unhappiness.
*Life doesn't have much meaning.
I believe there is some real purpose for my life.

Ellison, 1983; Miller *et al.*, 1998
(Items marked * are reverse-scored)

◆

In the study by Miller *et al.* (1998), African-Americans scored higher than Caucasian-Americans on overall spiritual well-being, and on the two sub-scales – religious and existential well-being. This is consistent with the view that African-Americans, like some other minority groups in Western society, are more religiously active, and value religion more highly, than do members of the dominant host culture (Loewenthal and Cinnirella, 1999b; Jacobson, 1997).

Trust and faith

Next in this review of 'typically' religious feelings which are positive, come trust and faith (also given some attention in chapter 4). 'Faith' is a term with a wide range of meanings. For example, Smith's (1979) definition of faith is that it is one's orientation or total response to oneself, to others, and to the universe. Here, however, I wish to refer to faith in the narrower sense of religious trust, expressed particularly in the face of adversity. This may have several components:

- closeness to God;
- a feeling that whatever happens is part of a divine plan, and is ultimately for the best even if this is not immediately apparent;
- a feeling that it is possible to bear whatever happens.

These feelings have been observed in a number of studies of people coping with different kinds of adversity (Gilbert, 1992; McIntosh *et al.*,

1993; Loewenthal, MacLeod, *et al.* 2000), and the evidence so far suggests that they may be helpful in coping with difficult life circumstances (Maton, 1989).

Other aspects of trust and faith are discussed in chapters 4 and 6. Here we shall concentrate on the emotional aspects. Pargament *et al.* (1988) have pointed out that people can vary in the extent and style of dependence on God. Apart from the people who feel no awareness of God, who claim to be non-believers, trust in God may involve:

- a total passivity – leaving everything to God, or
- a feeling of partnership with God, working together, or
- a feeling that God will only help those who help themselves.

Self-esteem

Another important kind of feeling which may be sometimes linked with religious factors is self-esteem. This can come from the feeling of belonging and being valued, both by one's religious group (Shams and Jackson, 1993), and by God (Hood, 1992). Issues to do with religion and self-esteem will be returned to at the end of chapter 6, when we look at the issue of religious identity.

NEGATIVE FEELINGS

We now turn to negative feelings in the religious context. One of the most interesting sets of questions in the psychology of religion is whether religion fosters feelings of guilt, shame and obsessionality, arising from anxiety over the need to be careful in maintaining religious rules. Are anxiety, guilt, shame and obsessionality more likely among the religious? If these negative emotions are encouraged by religion, does this mean that religion might lead to psychopathology (mental illness)? Perhaps, some would argue, we would be better off without the anxiety, guilt and other negative feelings associated with religious life?

Guilt, shame and anxiety

First, what do we mean by the terms guilt, shame and anxiety? (We will turn to obsessionality in the next section.)

Anxiety is 'an unpleasant emotional state' involving 'fear, with the anticipation of future evil' (English and English, 1958). Anxiety is a common emotion, and we should be careful to distinguish emotion from *psychopathology* (psychological illness or disorder). A person who feels

LIVERPOOL JOHN MOORES UNIVERSITY
LEARNING SERVICES

anxious is not necessarily ill at all. Psychological illness involves normal everyday emotions which have got out of hand, have become intense, persistent and uncontrollable. The anxiety disorders are a group of unpleasant conditions in which this has happened. As the term implies, anxiety is an important symptom. The anxiety disorders include phobias, panic disorder, obsessive-compulsive disorder, and generalized anxiety disorder.

Guilt involves the 'realization that one has violated ethical or moral or religious principles', while *shame* also involves a realization of a shortcoming or impropriety, of having acted in an unworthy manner (English and English, 1958). Shame may be more dependent on experiences of ridicule or criticism from others. Both shame and guilt are unpleasant, negative emotions following the transgression of moral standards. Tangney (1995; Tangney *et al.*, 1995) has suggested that guilt is a more healthy component of superego functioning: Guilt fosters empathy and reparative behaviour and is not associated with psychopathology. Shame is associated with several forms of psychopathology (including depression and anxiety), and with feelings of loss of control and a poor evaluation of the self.

Guilt and shame seem to be an integral feature of many, and perhaps all, religious traditions. Religion involves not only the idea of God, but of the ideas of right and wrong – divinely ordained rules about behaviour. For example:

> My earliest childhood memory of guilt as an all-pervasive aspect of life goes back to the confessional prayer that opened every service: '... we poor sinners confess unto Thee, that we are by nature sinful and unclean, and that we have sinned against Thee by thought, word and deed.'
>
> (Belgum, 1992)

> Forgive us, our Father, for we have sinned, pardon us, our King, for we have transgressed, for You are God who is good and forgives.
>
> (Translated from the Hebrew liturgical prayer recited three times daily.)

Internalized self-monitoring of actions, words and thoughts is not unique to religion, but it is part of religion, or at least part of Western religion. Psychologists have asked whether this induces a general sense of guilt, or shame, or low self-esteem, or excessive scrupulosity and obsessionality.

The relations between guilt, shame, self-esteem and religion are mixed. Guilt and shame tend to be associated – and to go along with depression, which in turn is associated with low self-esteem, but there are no simple associations with religiosity. Low self-esteem may go along with extrinsic religiosity (see chapter 6), and a view of God as punitive. High self-esteem may go along with intrinsic religiosity (see chapter 6) and a view of God as loving (Hood, 1992). Religious people may report higher levels of guilt, but this does not have a detrimental effect on mental health (Luyten *et al.*, 1998). Many of these findings are beset with problems to do with measurement.

Hood (1992) has concluded that there is empirical documentation of a paradoxical effect:

> '... in which guilt is stimulated by a punitive God, only to be forgiven in turn (especially in more fundamentalist Christian traditions) ... test items like "I am a hopeless sinner, but I am worthy in the sight of God" evoke what would otherwise be merely inappropriate guilt ("I am a sinner") and equally inappropriate pride ("I am worthy in the sight of God").'

Janoff-Bulman (1979) has distinguished between characterological self-blame, involving guilt and deservingness, and blame for actions. Self-blame for character failings ('I am a bad person, and it's my fault') *is* associated with depression, whereas self-blame for actions ('I did a bad thing, and it's my fault') is not. This distinction – which is important in studying the clinical implications of causal thinking – could be important in the religious context, in unravelling the clearly intricate relations between religion, and guilt, self-esteem and related factors. Also important is the conclusion by Tangney noted above, that it is shame rather than guilt that may have harmful effects on self-worth. It is useful to note that in the Luyten *et al.* (1998) study quoted above, guilt and empathy were associated with measures of religious belief and involvement, while shame was not. It is shame, rather than guilt, which is now thought to be associated with poorer mental health, and as we have seen, shame may not be strongly associated with religiosity.

Obsessionality

What about obsessionality? Is this fostered by religious practice? *Obsessions* are 'recurrent, persistent, irrational ideas, thoughts, images or impulses that are experienced not as voluntary but as unwanted invasions of consciousness'. *Obsessive–compulsive disorder* (OCD) is a common anxiety disorder, characterized by obsessions and (behavioural) compulsions. There is some evidence of an overall relationship with religion. There are overall associations between measures of religiosity and measures of obsessionality (Lewis, 1994; Lewis and Joseph, 1994; Lewis and Maltby, 1994), but this effect is problematic, and difficult to interpret. Does some aspect of religion cause obsessionality? Or are obsession-prone people drawn to religious practice? Or does religious involvement somehow give the appearance of obsessionality, as when Islam and Judaism encourage frequent ritual washing?

In a recent review article, Lewis (1998) reached an interesting conclusion. Lewis pointed out that it was necessary to distinguish between obsessional *personality*, characterized by *traits* such as orderliness, rigidity and (over-) emphasis on hygiene and self-control, and obsessional *neurosis*, characterized by *symptoms* such as compulsive thoughts, ritualistic behaviour and guilt (Fontana, 1980). Most of the studies reviewed by Lewis involved student populations from Christian backgrounds. His conclusions are interesting: in spite of some conflict, generally, religiosity is associated with obsessional *traits*, but not with obsessional neurosis. For instance, of twenty-two studies looking at the relations between religious attitudes or religious practice, and obsessional personality, eleven found a significant relationship. By contrast, of nine studies looking at the relationship between religious attitudes or religious practice, and obsessional symptoms, only three reported a significant relationship, and there were no significant relationships reported between religious attitudes and obsessional *symptoms*. Interpreting this to answer the question raised in the previous paragraph – perhaps religion may encourage behaviour that can seem obsessional, but perhaps it does not attract or foster obsessional neurosis.

The relationship is not a simple one. As stated, it is important to distinguish obsessionality, a character or personality trait, from the pathological manifestations of extreme obsessionality in obsessive–compulsive disorder (OCD). Greenberg *et al.* (1987) have discussed the issue of whether the scruples encouraged by religion might lead to mistaken diagnosis, and came to the conclusion that cases of excessive religious scrupulosity were recognized as excessive, both by sufferers, and by their friends, family and religious advisers.

◆

Martin Luther is said to have struggled with scruples about his failure to achieve justification (freedom from the penalty of sin). Luther would repeat a confession and to be sure of including everything, would review his entire life until the confessor grew weary and exclaimed: 'Man, God is not angry with you, you are angry with God. Don't you know that God commands you to hope?'

Bainton, 1950; Erikson, 1958; Greenberg *et al.* 1987

◆

Greenberg and Witztum (1994) have compared obsessional behaviour with a religious content, derived from a religious concern, with obsessional behaviour by religiously-observant patients which is unrelated to religious concerns, such as repeatedly checking whether a door was locked. Greenberg and Witztum believe that religion may provide the setting for the expression of scrupulosity, but may play no direct causal role. One observation which supports this is that 'religious' obsessional behaviour is confined to specific areas (prayer, ritual cleanliness, and dietary laws, among Jewish patients). There are many other areas in which equally great care is enjoined by religious law, but these do not provide a forum for obsessionality. Religion may provide a setting for obsessional behaviour, but may not play a direct causal role.

◆

Ezekiel is 28, married with two children. The bar mitzvah at thirteen years of age represents the passing into manhood, when the Jewish male becomes responsible for his own religious practice. At this time he started spending excessive time in prayer and its preparations. His prayers took up to three hours daily, about three times longer than his peers. Despite the time spent, the content was abbreviated, the less important part being omitted, so that the significant sections could be said at the correct time. Some sections would be repeated many times, because he feared he had improper thoughts. He had read that one should be clean at all orifices before prayers. He therefore spent twenty minutes before each of the three daily prayers cleaning and checking his anal region, which caused him to arrive late for prayers, so that he always missed the important sections. He considered his rituals excessive, but experienced no resistance in carrying them out. He said he would continue to put up with them, but his wife was contemplating divorce.

(Greenberg *et al.* 1987)

◆

Religious OCD symptoms may be particularly hard to treat, since the sufferer may claim a special, sacred status for these symptoms (Greenberg and Witztum, 1991). In an interesting paper, Greenberg (1997) examined some of the special properties of religious OCD symptoms. He compared religious and other OCD symptoms in a sample of fourteen sufferers from OCD, all of whom were orthodox Jewish. Greenberg started by suggesting that religious and compulsive rituals had similar features.

Table 5.3   A comparison of religious ritual and compulsive ritual (based on Greenberg, 1997)

Religious ritual	Compulsive ritual
May be repetitive	Repetitive
Must be performed in a certain way	Performed in a certain way
Precision is laudable	Precision reduces anxiety
Omission is sinful	Omission increases anxiety
Common topics: cleanliness, sex	Common topics: cleanliness, sex, precision

In Table 5.3, Greenberg is comparing religious rituals which are not compulsive, just rituals prescribed by religion, such as praying at particular times and in particular ways, fasting at certain times, eating certain foods, washing and other cleaning activities. Like Freud (1907) at the beginning of the century, Greenberg noted important similarities between religiously-prescribed acts, and neurotic obsessional actions. Greenberg noted a key feature of compulsive rituals, which are that they are normally perceived by the sufferer as:

- excessive;
- unreasonable;
- distressing;
- interfering with daily functioning.

Greenberg thought that where compulsive rituals were *also* religious, the sufferer might perceive these symptoms as having a special status, compared to other symptoms. Religious symptoms might be associated with less distress and less resistance, and they might be perceived as more logical. Greenberg thought therefore that more time would be spent carrying out religious OCD symptoms compared to other symptoms. In fact religious symptoms compared to other symptoms were seen as similarly distressing and illogical. There were also a number of other similarities, for example in age of onset, willingness to seek help, and type of help seen as appropriate. However, religious patients reported spending twice as long carrying out their religious ritual symptoms compared to other symptoms. Most religious symptoms were concerned with cleanliness, and with prayer (repetition because the patient feared that their concentration had been inadequate).

This offers some evidence that religious symptoms may be harder to deal with than other symptoms. Greenberg and Witztum say that liaison with religious authorities may be essential in the treatment of religious OCD symptoms, since a religious authority figure can discourage the practice of religious symptoms. If the psychiatrist or psychologist were to do this, he or she would be seen as threatening the client's religious values.

In brief, there are mixed relationships between religion on the one hand, and guilt and obsessionality on the other. However, recent evidence and interpretations have suggested that religion may not in this case foster *psychopathological* guilt or obsessionality, even though it may sometimes *appear* to do so.

RELIGION AND PSYCHOPATHOLOGY

Having considered whether religious factors might be important in causing obsessive compulsive disorders, we now turn to the best-known and most common forms of psychopathology: first, the 'common cold' of psychopathology, depression – often associated with anxiety and self-harm; second, forms of psychosis, schizophrenia and paranoid illnesses, which inevitably brings up the question of whether beliefs about demons and evil spirits are a sign of madness.

Depression and madness have both been linked with religion, but as we saw with guilt and related feelings, the theoretical and empirical links are complicated. Instead of trying to give a comprehensive survey, which could be long and probably tedious, I will pick out a few themes from the enormous literature on religion and psychopathology.

Depression

Depression can be an appropriate and non-pathological mood state, in response to a loss or similar saddening event. It is unpleasant, but not in itself an illness. However, if the negative mood state persists and becomes uncontrollable, a depressive illness may ensue. Depressive illnesses are characterized by a prolonged low mood, which cannot be lifted, and several other unpleasant symptoms which might include:

- hopelessness and pessimistic thoughts;
- despondency and lethargy;
- disturbances of sleep, eating and sexual functioning;

- loss of interest;
- other physical and mental symptoms.

The average person has an approximately one in ten chance of suffering from a depressive illness at some point in their life. That means that depressive illness is quite commonly experienced.

There is an overwhelming mass of evidence that, generally, religion is likely to be associated with better mental health, including lower levels of depression (Bergin, 1983; Loewenthal, 1995; Worthington *et al.*, 1996). This is unlikely to be a simple effect. Religion does not in and of itself cause better mental health. Some features associated with religion may help to promote better mental health. Some features associated with religion may have the opposite effect.

Here is a list of some of the ways in which religious factors may raise or lower levels of mental illness:

- features of life-style in religious groups may affect levels and types of stress, which in turn may affect levels of depression and possibly other mental illnesses;
- several features of religion have been suggested to have a stress-buffering effect. Such features include prayer and faith, which may help the person to feel better about the situation ('God is taking care of me', 'God is helping me to cope with all this')(Loewenthal, MacLeod, *et al.*, 2000) (see also the discussions in chapter 3 on prayer [pages 34–38], and in chapter 6, [pages 128–131] on religious coping);
- people in religious groups may receive better social support. This in turn can help to alleviate the depressing effects of severe stress;
- other features of religion may make people feel worse about their suffering ('God has let me down, maybe I am a bad person'), although empirically this does not seem to be a salient effect;
- religious factors can have other less direct effects on mental health. For example, religious rules forbidding suicide may lower suicide rates, resulting in more live depressed people in the population.

Examples of some of these effects follow. They are also discussed in chapters 3 and 6.

Living in a closed social group in which religious observance is normative can affect patterns of stress, which in turn can affect psychiatric disorder (see Figure 5.1).

Figure 5.1 *How the forms and norms of religion can affect emotions and psychopathology: the examples of depression and anxiety among Jews and Christians. (Loewenthal, Goldblatt, Gorton et al. 1997a, 1997b; Loewenthal, Goldblatt and Lubitsh, 1998).*

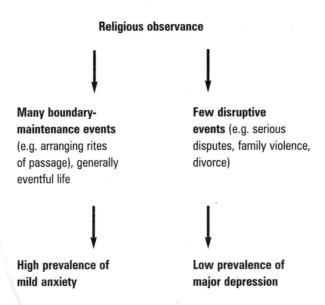

Interestingly, in most cultural groups major depression is more likely among women than among men. However, studies in Israel, the USA and the UK have shown that Jewish men are as likely to suffer from major depression as Jewish women (Levav *et al.*, 1993; Loewenthal *et al.*, 1995; Levav *et al.*, 1997). Two possible factors which might explain this are:

- suicide rates are lower in cultural-religious groups (such as Jews and Muslims) which do not endorse or encourage suicide (Ineichen, 1997);
- alcohol may be less often used by Jewish men as a way of coping with depression.

Thus one hypothesis is that more Jewish men appear to be depressed because they are less likely to be alcoholic and they are less likely to have killed themselves (see Figure 5.2).

Does religion in fact deter from suicide? The most famous suggestion to this effect was advanced by Durkheim (1952), who thought that some

Figure 5.2.   Why men may be less likely than women to appear to be depressed (based on Loewenthal et al., 1995)

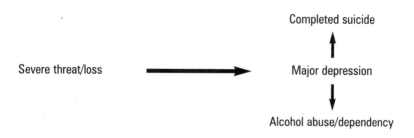

forms of suicide might be inhibited by the effects of forms of social organization associated with religion.

Ineichen (1997) has suggested that suicide rates might be lower in cultures in which there are strong religious prohibitions against suicide. Ineichen specifically contrasted suicide rates in Hindu and Muslim groups in different countries. Islamic teaching is generally more strongly against suicide than are the Hindu scriptures. Suicide rates are generally lower in Muslim groups than among Hindus. Jahangir *et al.* (1998) studied 118 psychiatric outpatients suffering from depression. All were refugees from Afghanistan, then in Pakistan, and who were Muslim. Each patient was rated for religiosity, and on three suicide-related factors: suicide plans, suicide attempts, and wish for death. There were consistent (significant) relationships between religiosity, and lower levels of suicide plans, suicide attempts and wish for death. In another study comparing Hindus and Muslims, Kamal and Loewenthal (2002) asked Muslims and Hindus living in Britain to complete the Reasons for Living Inventory (Linehan *et al.*, 1983). This measure asks participants to endorse reasons for which they might stay alive if they were thinking of killing themselves.

There are six distinct clusters of reasons:

- survival and coping (e.g. 'I believe I can find other solutions to my problems');
- responsibility to family (e.g. 'My family depends on me and needs me');
- child-related concerns (e.g. 'The effect on my children would be harmful');

- fear of suicide (e.g. 'I am afraid of the act of killing myself, the pain, the blood, the violence');
- fear of social disapproval (e.g. 'Other people would think I am weak and selfish');
- moral (religious) objections (e.g. 'My religious beliefs forbid it').

In this study, the two religious groups obtained very similar scores on four scales, but the Muslims were slightly higher than the Hindus on responsibility to family, and very markedly higher than the Hindus on moral (religious) objections.

This chain of evidence suggests that religious rules can affect people's beliefs about suicide, and their actual behaviour.

As far as religion and depression are concerned, the relationships are quite complicated, but the net effect is that there is, as stated, a general association between higher religiosity and lower depression.

Psychosis and the demon problem

Psychosis is a 'gross impairment of psychological functioning, including loss of self-insight and of contact with reality, such as is found in mental disorders involving hallucinations and delusions' (Lazarus and Coleman, 1995). The most common psychotic illness is *schizophrenia*, which affects about one person in every 200. Although this term literally means 'split mind', schizophrenia should not be confused with multiple-personality disorder, a dissociative neurotic illness in which the sufferer may switch from one personality to another, as in the very famous literary example of Dr Jekyll and Mr Hyde. Schizophrenia involves incoherent thought, and often incoherent speech, feelings may seem 'flat' or inappropriate, social functioning is poor, and the sufferer does not care well for him or herself. Hallucinations and delusions are common. Psychotic illnesses are generally considered more serious than neurotic illnesses (the anxiety disorders and most forms of depressive illness). They are more difficult to live with, and sufferers are often less likely to be able to function normally in work and social relationships than are sufferers from neurotic illnesses. Biological and neuropsychological factors are probably much more important in causing psychotic illnesses, and stress relatively less important, than is the case with neurotic illnesses.

A difficult problem confronting most psychiatrists at some point in their career is how to decide when a belief or experience is psychotic or a bone fide religious belief or delusion (Littlewood and Lipsedge, 1989; Loewenthal, 1999).

◆

THE AFRO-CARIBBEAN SCHIZOPHRENIA PROBLEM: WHEN NORMATIVE EMOTIONS ARE SEEN BY OTHERS AS PSYCHOPATHOLOGY

Schizophrenia has a higher prevalence among Afro-Caribbeans in the UK and the USA, compared to its prevalence among other cultural groups in the UK and the USA, *and* compared to its prevalence among Afro-Caribbeans in African and Caribbean countries. Littlewood and Lipsedge (1989) noted that it can be difficult to diagnose psychopathology in the culturally alien. They noted (1981) that many cases of schizophrenia among Afro-Caribbeans in London had a 'religious flavour'. It is possible that religious 'symptoms' may sometimes cause over-diagnosis of schizophrenia among Afro-Caribbeans (Loewenthal and Cinnirella, 1999b). For example, belief in spirit possession is normative in many societies. But a patient who insists that they have been bewitched, and are suffering from stomach pains caused by a hex placed on them by an enemy, may be regarded as paranoid or schizophrenic by a Western psychiatrist.

◆

One example is offered by Fulford (1999). Fulford describes a forty-year-old black American professional man, 'Simon', a lawyer, from a Baptist background. This man had experienced occasional psychic experiences, which he used to discuss with his religious adviser, a man he consulted about major life events and decisions. More recently, Simon has been extremely troubled since a group of colleagues have brought a lawsuit against him. The complaint is unfounded, but it would be extremely expensive and risky to fight this. Simon took to praying at an altar set up in his living room at home. He discovered that the candles he lit to accompany his prayers dripped wax onto his bible, and he felt that the words marked by the wax had a special significance. Most people he showed this bible to, were not impressed, but Simon persisted in saying that the marked words had special symbolism, and that he was chosen and marked out for special responsibility by God. He also felt that often his thoughts were interrupted by sudden 'thought insertion' from a higher source. Fulford reports that he has presented Simon's case in a number of training seminars, and has asked pairs of trainees working together to offer a diagnosis. Most commonly, schizophrenia or schizo-affective disorder are the diagnoses offered. When asked what the diagnosis is based on, most trainees respond that there is a clear first-rank symptom of schizophrenia, namely the deluded perception of meaning in the drippings of the wax candles. Another possible symptom is suggested by the 'thought insertions'. Fulford goes on to describe how Simon's religious experiences and feelings gave him the strength to carry on, and to fight and win the lawsuit. He felt vindicated, he gained confidence in combating racism, his prestige as a lawyer was enhanced, and his legal practice flourished. His religious experiences continued. He used some of the money gained from the lawsuit to start a charitable foundation. He began working for the reconciliation of Christianity and Islam. When this sequel to Simon's story is revealed, most trainees retract their former diagnosis, suggesting that perhaps it was a benign form of schizophrenia. Or, suggests Fulford, an adaptive religious experience? Fulford is able to argue that older diagnostic schemes would label Simon as schizophrenic, since he does have a first-rank symptom of schizophrenia, or schizo-affective disorder. However, the American Psychiatric Association's current diagnostic manual (DSM-IV) does allow the distinction to be made, between a 'symptom', and a religious experience, and for a diagnosis to be made under this scheme, there must be deterioration in some other area of behaviour, such as work, social relationships, or self-care. Simon showed no such deterioration. Fulford's example shows how easy it can be to construe religious behaviour and beliefs as signs of madness.

Religious beliefs can seem bizarre, and may give the appearance of madness. The most interesting beliefs for our present topic are beliefs in evil spirits, demons and the like. In many, indeed most cultures, demons or evil spirits may be seen as cause of harm, including physical and mental health problems (Lewis, 1971; Dein, 1996; Bainbridge, 1997). In Switzerland, Pfeifer studied 343 out-patients in a psychiatric clinic. Over one-third thought their mental health problems could have been caused by the influence of evil spirits, labelling this as 'occult bondage' or 'possession', and nearly one-third had sought help for deliverance through ritual prayers and exorcism. In Israel, Youngman et al. (1999) observed that belief in spiritual factors as causes of mental and physical illness was normative among Ethiopian immigrants. However, environmental and personality factors were also seen as causes of disorder. Spiritual causes of disorder were 'Zar' (spirit possession), curses and the evil eye. Interestingly, in the Youngman et al. study, the Ethiopians interviewed thought that depression-related symptoms were much more serious than psychotic symptoms. The latter were seen as caused by 'Zar' (spirit possession), and apparently not thought of as particularly pathological. One interviewee said, 'I have been with them (Zar) my whole life.'

◆

A famous mid-nineteenth-century case involved Louisa Nottidge, from a wealthy East Anglian family (Schwieso, 1996). Louisa was from a culturally dominant and privileged background, and her story highlights the difficulties that a religious enthusiast may have to contend with, even without the difficulties of being 'alien'. Louisa was inspired by a fervent local Anglican curate, whose views became unorthodox. Louisa and others followed him to join his millenarian religious sect, the Agapemone. Louisa's family tracked her down, kidnapped her and had her certified as insane on the grounds that she had '... estranged herself from her mother's house ... to follow a person ... whom she believed to be Almighty God, and herself immortal'. She was confined to a private asylum whose proprietor asked the Commissioners in Lunacy to examine her. There were a number of visits, and numerous reports on Louisa in the commission's minutes. The commission agreed with the certifying doctors that Louisa was suffering from 'religious monomania'. Louisa in confinement was depressed, but '... walked up and down singing what she termed praises, making use of no intelligible words'. As time passed she cheered up, and managed to contact the Agapemonites, who mounted a campaign for her release. Release was ordered by the Commissioners in Lunacy, who declared that '... her extraordinary and irrational opinions on religion ... were irreconcilable ... with soundness of mind', but that apart from her religious opinions, she was competent, calm and rational. Louisa rejoined the Agapemonites and started proceedings against her family for trespass and false imprisonment. The family's defence council sought to expose all the ludicrous, unusual and unconventional aspects of life in the Agapemonite community. Louisa won her case since the presiding judge told the Lunacy Commissioners that they had no right to confine anyone 'safe and harmless', regardless of their religious opinions. However, popular sympathy was clearly with Louisa's family, and with the derisory amount of the damages awarded to Louisa. Note that Louisa was considered 'competent, calm and rational' – apart from her religious opinions.

◆

Peters *et al.* (1999) marshal the arguments that 'certain groups of people have similar experiences to the positive symptoms of schizophrenia' (notably delusions) 'but remain functioning members of society, such as those with profound religious experiences (Jackson and Fulford, 1997)'.

Peters *et al.* compared members of two types of religious groups (New Religious Movements or NRMs, and Christians) with non-religious people, and with psychotic patients suffering from delusions. The NRM members were drawn from the Hare Krishna group and a Pagan order (Druids). Two measures of delusional thinking were used in this study (which included factors such as persecution, paranormal beliefs and religiosity). The main findings and conclusions from this study were:

- Individuals from the NRMs scored higher than the Christians and the non-religious on the delusions measures, and similarly to the deluded, psychotic group; this included a measure of 'florid, psychotic symptoms ... rarely endorsed in the normal population' (the Delusions Symptoms-State Inventory, DSSI, Foulds and Bedford, 1975);
- NRM members were however less distressed and preoccupied by their delusional experiences than were the psychotic patients;
- The Christians did not score higher than the non-religious did on the delusions measures, which suggests that religious beliefs *per se* do not account for delusional thinking.

These findings led Peters *et al.* to conclude that delusional beliefs in themselves need not be symptomatic of psychosis, or even of 'schizotypy' (psychosis-proneness: Claridge, 1994). They suggest that diagnosis of illness must be guided by *form* rather than *content*: 'It is not *what* you believe, but *how* you believe it'.

We have seen that belief in spirit possession is quite common, and that two effects are possible. One is that spirit possession can be seen as a matter of course, and not as disturbing as other forms of disorder. Sometimes it may not be seen as disordered at all. Another effect is that 'bizarre' religious beliefs, including beliefs in spirit possession, may in themselves be taken as a sign of psychological disorder by (Western) professionals who do not share these beliefs. Let us not forget, however, that there are countless examples of mental illness, often psychotic, in which the patient's belief that he or she is being possessed or persecuted by malign spiritual forces plays a key role. In the box below, for example, is a case history offering a vivid illustration of religious visions of a persecuting angel, following grief and guilt after the death of the client's father. It illustrates the therapists' awareness and use of the client's religious idioms.

◆

Ezra was a twenty-four-year-old married man who had been a Jewish penitent for two years. He was brought by his brother to the clinic because of 'bizarre behaviour'. During the previous six months, while Ezra had been immersed in studying the Zohar (the key Jewish mystical text), he had heard voices and had dreams in which his late father appeared as a threatening black apparition. Ezra engaged in ascetic practices: he fasted frequently, wore tattered clothes, and visited the graves of Zaddikim (Jewish saints). He lit ritual candles on these graves, and at home. After the birth of his first child, a girl, these practices became more intense, and four months later he was brought by his brother to the clinic and admitted. Ezra appeared unkempt, and was not completely oriented to place and time. His co-operation was minimal. He was depressed in mood, but his formal thinking was normal. He reported visions of a personal angel, and also nightmares in which his father appeared, dressed in black and with a sad, suffering face. These visions and nightmares had started after the birth of his daughter.

Ezra was the younger of two sons of North African descent. His father had been a quiet, sad man, who had begun drinking in mid-life, and had become a chronic alcoholic. At home, he would drink himself to oblivion, and fall asleep in his own vomit. One night, when Ezra was fifteen, the father called Ezra to bring him a glass of water. Ezra brought the water, but when his father asked him to stay with him, Ezra refused. In the morning, the father was found dead.

Ezra became depressed and guilt-ridden, blaming himself for his father's death. He began taking hard drugs. His brother persuaded him to quit drugs, and to join the army, which he did. After two years' military service, Ezra left the army, became religiously observant and married. He prayed for a boy to name after his father.

When Ezra's daughter was born, he was shocked. He began to hear a voice, which he identified as belonging to his personal angel. The angel said that instead of protecting him, he was punishing him for the neglect that lead to his father's death. The angel told him to fast, wear tattered clothes, visit the graves of saints, abstain from sexual relations, and generally to afflict himself. Then he might be forgiven.

In therapy, the therapists suggested to Ezra that in Jewish law, it is forbidden to mourn a dead relative for more than a year. They appreciated that he was seeking an ecstatic religious experience which would signify that he had been forgiven, and attempted to encourage this, for example by asking him to bring his father's photograph to sessions. Ezra wrote a letter to his father asking for forgiveness, and also looked intently at his father's picture in a therapeutic session, and began to weep. The therapists also asked Ezra to investigate the angel: what were its intentions? What was its name? Was it really an evil spirit in disguise? In the thirteenth session, the therapists, together with Ezra's brother who was a religious authority, attempted to exorcize the angel. Leading the ritual, the brother asked one of the therapists to read a formula from the mystical-magical work *The Book of the Angel Raziel*, which Ezra used to summon the angel. During the reading, Ezra began to sway, moving his body and head in an increasingly rhythmic and vigorous manner. He added his own ecstatic sing-song of a two-syllable phrase, and seemed to enter a trance. Suddenly he became quiet and informed the others that the angel was present. Ezra's brother informed the angel that on behalf of the religious court, he was ordering the angel to leave, and to return no more, neither for good, nor for bad, not even to reveal mystical secrets. Ezra seemed stunned and confused, because of the long, intense, ambivalent relationship with the angel. One of the therapists explained that from then on, the angel had no right to disturb him because the angel belonged to another realm. The brother, tense and emotional, told Ezra to complete the exorcism by blowing out the candles. Ezra did this, and he was declared a free man, under his own control.

The therapists had intended to convert the angel from a punitive enemy, to an ego-supportive ally. Ezra's brother had thwarted this intention, by his statement that the angel must not return again, for good or for bad. However, ultimately, the angel behaved according to the therapists' expectations by returning occasionally, always in the role of an ally.

Described in Witztum *et al.*, 1990a

Another study offering helpful descriptions of spirit possession is by Ensinck and Robertson (1999). They conducted a series of interviews in the Xhosa language, in South Africa, with sixty-two African psychiatric patients and their families. The participants in this study had all used the 'Western' psychiatric services, and were generally satisfied – or at least that is what they said to the interviewer, who was identified as coming from the hospital! Many had also used:

- herbalists – there was general satisfaction here;
- faith healers – here there were mixed feelings, mostly uncertain about satisfaction;
- diviners – widespread dissatisfaction.

The two commonest indigenous classification categories of psychological disturbance were *amafufunyana* – possession by evil spirits – and *ukuphambana* – madness (see boxes below). A mixture of psychosocial causes (stress), religious causes (God's will) and indigenous causes were usually seen as underlying the disorder.

---◆---

A CASE OF SPIRIT POSSESSION (AMAFUFUNYANA)

Patricia is a twenty-three-year-old student who lives with her aunt, a domestic worker. Patricia's aunt said that Patricia's problems started when she was studying for a mathematics examination. She took off her clothes in public and was brought home by community members. She also became promiscuous when she was sick. The aunt said, 'She claimed she was raped, but she was used by the *amafufunyana* to do evil things.' She was admitted to a psychiatric hospital for about one month and was diagnosed as having a bipolar affective disorder (manic-depression). Patricia's aunt believes that the problem is caused by bewitchment, because 'there are things that speak inside her, saying who sent the *amafufunyana* to her', and 'the reason is jealousy, nothing else'. The bewitchment was said to involve 'doing magic, like mixing grave soil and ants into food'. She also thought that worry contributed to the illness. Patricia's aunt was uncertain whether she was satisfied with the hospital treatment. 'The problem is that we did not ask the name of the illness, because we are illiterate, and we do not know the name the white doctors are telling us. We took everything for granted. White doctors do not know how to cure illnesses caused by blacks. The only thing they can cure is TB. The *amafufunyana* want to be taken out by black people'. After discharge from hospital, Patricia was taken to a diviner and given traditional medicines including a purgative and an emetic, but she refused to stay with the diviner and drink the medicine. The aunt was dissatisfied with the treatment of the diviner. She said, 'The problem is that the diviners are liars, because she promised to take out the *amafufunyana*, but never did. Patricia still ran naked afterwards.' Patricia was then taken to a faith healer where she stayed for one month. He did not name the illness. He used prayer and holy water. Her aunt reported 'They said the *amafufunyana* are out of her, all five came out.' (Ensinck and Robertson do not report on Patricia's behaviour at the time of the interview, following treatment by the faith healer.)

Ensinck and Robertson, 1999

MADNESS (UKUPHAMBANA)

Sipho is thirty years old, unemployed, and lives with his mother who is a pensioner. Sipho's mother said that he withdrew from people, and began to talk and laugh when alone. He became very fearful, and wanted to run away. Sipho's mother feared he would run under a car. She thinks Sipho's illness was caused by drug abuse, and believes that he is poisoned through his drugs by evil spirits. She also believes that the drugs affect the functioning of his brain. He was in hospital for ten days, and was diagnosed as suffering from alcoholic hallucinosis.

Sipho's mother said that she was satisfied with the hospital treatment. The illness was explained to her, and after the treatment Sipho stopped wanting to run in front of cars. However, Sipho's mother thought that there were too few nurses to look after the patients. Before going to hospital they had consulted a diviner. A huge sum of money was paid, amounting to one-third of Sipho's mother's annual income. The diviner saw Sipho once only, and gave him medicine to drink and to wash with. The mother was very dissatisfied, and felt she had been cheated and robbed by the diviner.

Ensinck and Robertson, 1999

◆

This section on psychosis in relation to religion has been particularly concerned with the interesting relationships between psychotic illness, and beliefs in spirit possession. We have seen that there are several important effects, namely that belief in spirit possession is quite widespread. It may be seen as a cause of madness, but it may be seen as a state independent of madness. Beliefs in spirit possession and similar phenomena may be held by perfectly normal-functioning individuals and are not necessarily symptoms of psychosis at all. When a sufferer from psychosis believes that he or she is being possessed or persecuted by malign spiritual forces, this is very distressing and preoccupying, and religious/spiritual means may be helpful in relieving the sufferer.

SUMMARY

This chapter looked first at the theory and evidence on the early origins of religious feelings. Then some characteristically religious pleasant emotions: mystical awe, trust and faith, and some of the factors associated with them were examined. Freudian, object-relations and attachment theory were described. Negative feelings, particularly guilt, shame, anxiety and obsessionality were examined, and the question asked whether religion might foster these negative feelings, and even illness resulting from them. Finally we turned to the best-known and common forms of psychological illness – depression, and psychosis. Religious factors in causing and alleviating depression were examined. Psychosis was examined particularly in relation to beliefs about spirit possession.

6 HOW RELIGION CAN AFFECT BEHAVIOUR, THOUGHT AND FEELING

In this chapter we examine some of the ways in which religion might affect behaviour, thought and feeling in areas that are not explicitly religious. We examine three areas. First, *morality*: might religion make people 'better' or 'worse' in terms of everyday goodness? Second, *personal happiness and distress*: how might aspects of religion contribute to overall feelings of well-being or unhappiness? And finally, *prejudice*: does religion make people more or less tolerant, more or less racist, more or less humane?

Thus, generally, does religion make people better people, and happier people?

THE MORAL CONTROL OF BEHAVIOUR

Morality

What is morality? How does it relate to religion? And how does it relate to behaviour? Thus the question is whether and how religion affects behaviour, via morality:

Religion ⟶ Morality ⟶ Behaviour

Morality involves ethical standards of behaviour, the evaluation of intentions and behaviour as right or wrong, good or bad. Moral standards can be rooted in religious tradition, and moral laws can be seen as having a divine origin. But, certainly in the Western world, morality and ethics can be seen as independent of religion. One of the best-known moral codes is the biblical Ten Commandments. These enjoin obviously religious duties, such as loving and worshipping God, as well as social and civil duties, such as not stealing and not committing adultery, and seeing that we and our families and employees take a weekly break from work. There is also a plea for self-control over thinking: not envying other people their possessions and partners.

Brown (1965) and others have been careful to distinguish between moral *behaviour*, moral *feeling*, and moral *thought*. Each could be independent of the other.

◆

Helen was looking at the photographs from her wedding. They were taken by a professional photographer, and for a suitable professional fee, he had supplied her with an album of proofs which showed the whole sequence of things that happened, featuring all the friends and relations who had come for the happy event. Included in the photographer's fee was a souvenir album for Helen and her husband, to be made up of enlargements of a selection of a small number of pictures chosen by the couple. Helen wanted to send souvenirs to her close friends and family, perhaps two or three pictures each, one of the friend or relation concerned, one of her and her husband, and one of a group of friends or relations including the friend or relation concerned. Helen's problem was that the prices charged by the photographer for copies and enlargements were much higher than the prices charged through the local photography enlargement service. She and her husband were very short of money, and needed every penny for rent and groceries. However, Helen felt that it would be more honest to order the photographs through the photographer. She felt it would be cheating him to have the copies made more cheaply elsewhere. Helen's friend told her not to be silly, that no one pays those ridiculous prices that the photographers charge. Helen's mother told her not to bother sending photographic souvenirs to people. She said that most people who came to the wedding brought their own cameras anyway. If they want photographs from the professional photographer, let them pay for it themselves. But Helen thought there would be people who would really appreciate the gift she had in mind: her grandparents, an elderly single friend and a young cousin who had come from abroad. She knew they had not brought their own camera, and it would not be appropriate to ask them to pay for photographs. She also knew that for each of them, the wedding had been a big event that they had looked forward to, and that they had planned coming for months. She had been deeply touched by how happy they were for her and her husband. In the end Helen ordered one medium-size photo for each of them from the photographer, featuring a group of friends or relatives, and including the friend or relation and Helen and her husband. She hoped they did not think she was being mean; but if they did, Helen felt that was better than knowing she had cheated the photographer of his rightful business.

◆

In the example above, Helen had a wealth of choices. These ranged from doing nothing, through to sending large sets of large photos to large numbers of friends and relations. She had to balance conflicting demands and feelings, and make moral choices about business ethics, overspending, and showing appreciation, and respecting the sensitivities of her friends and relations, and of the photographer. Her *behaviour* (what she actually did), her *thinking* (which included running through all the possibilities she could think of, and their justification), and her *feelings*, can all be seen as separate but interwoven strands, and as in most human dilemmas, there are conflicts between each.

Brown (1965) suggested that (moral, and other) behaviour, thought and feeling are acquired by different types of learning process:

- *Behaviour* is acquired by *operant learning*, epitomized by the training situation in which an animal or human learns to do something by a process of being rewarded for desirable behaviour. No language need necessarily be involved: a hungry rat will learn to thread its way through an intricate maze with increasing skill, to reach the food at the end.

- *Thought* is acquired by *cognitive learning*, often (but not always) involving language, always involving processes of symbolic, abstract representation.

- *Feelings* are acquired by *classical conditioning*, a process thought to be beyond cognitive control. Sharply unpleasant or pleasant stimuli are paired with a specific 'neutral' event – and afterwards there is a persistent and uncontrollable return of the strong feeling caused by the stimulus, whenever the previously neutral event recurs. A parent shouting a warning to a young child, or pulling them back, as they are about to run into the road after a ball is an example. This is likely to cause twinges of anxiety in future when stepping into a road. Sometimes the feelings may be excessive and inappropriate, as in agoraphobia, when the sufferer is terrified and paralysed by panic at the thought of going out of doors.

In this section of this chapter, we will examine some perspectives on morality, to try and untangle some of the ways in which religion might affect behaviour via morality.

Moral development

In discussing theories about the development of thinking and feeling in chapters 4 and 5, an overview was taken of the theories of Kohlberg and of Freud. We revisit these theories briefly, along with some others, in looking at moral development.

Kohlberg's impetus was the work of Piaget, particularly his stage theory of cognitive development. Kohlberg had felt that Piaget's own work on moral development did not do justice to the changes in the quality of moral thought that occurred in later childhood, adolescence and adulthood. Piaget had detected a very interesting shift in the quality of moral reasoning, however, in childhood. The kind of Piagetian dilemma that children were asked to discuss is described in the box below.

Ann's mother had a beautiful set of china that was stored in a glass-fronted cabinet. She had warned Ann never to take the china out of its cabinet. It should not be played with, as her mother would be very upset if any pieces were broken. Ann was longing to play with the china, however, and one day while her mother was busy upstairs, Ann quietly took a few pieces of china out to look at. Then she was tempted to play with them, just a little. Suddenly Ann heard footsteps on the stairs. Her mother was coming down. Quickly, Ann put the china back. But in her haste, one cup fell down and broke.

Joan's mother also had a beautiful set of china that was stored in a glass-fronted cabinet. She had also warned her daughter that she should never take the china out of its cabinet, for the same reason. However, one day there were some special visitors and Joan's mother decided to get out the special china set in honour of the occasion. After the visitors were gone, she said that she thought Joan could be trusted to dry the china and put it back in the cabinet. Joan was pleased, and proudly dried each piece after her mother had washed it, and placed everything on a tray, and carried it carefully towards the cabinet. Just then the cat darted past under Joan's feet – she tripped and the tray went flying. All six of the cups were broken.

Who was naughtier, Ann or Joan?

A. Joan was more naughty because she broke more cups than Ann did.
B. Ann was more naughty because she disobeyed her mother. Joan was not naughty because she was trying to help and the cups were broken by accident.

(Adapted from Piaget, 1932)

Younger children, under about the age of seven, usually give answers of type A, while older children give answers of type B. The first type of answer involves judging the badness of an action in terms of its *physical consequences*. Using this criterion, children will judge 'tall stories' told as jokes or fantasy as worse than 'small lies' told to deliberately deceive, because the distortion of truth is greater. Older children will judge in terms of psychological criteria – intentions: a lie is worse than a joke or a fantasy because there is intent to deceive. This shift from heteronomous to autonomous morality was an important observation by Piaget, and laid the foundation for Kohlberg's observations of changes in the quality of moral thought in later childhood and adulthood.

As described in chapter 4, Kohlberg detailed six stages in the development of moral thought, with two stages at each of three levels: *preconventional*, *conventional* and *post-conventional*. Fowler later related Kohlberg's stages to stages in the development of faith. Piaget, Kohlberg and Fowler are all concerned with *thought*, and this might be totally independent of behaviour. There have been empirical studies of moral thought, which have shown that on the whole, those whose moral reasoning is on a higher level are more likely to behave 'better' than those whose moral reasoning is on a lower level. Rest (1979, 1983) has developed a test of moral reasoning, which is a simpler method of assessing levels of moral reasoning than the extended interviews used by Kohlberg. Scores on Rest's Defining Issues Test have some relationship to behaviour both among adolescents and adults (Blasi, 1980). For example, those with convictions of criminal offences tend to have lower scores than those without criminal offence records.

How does Rest's test relate to religion? Members of fundamentalist Christian groups show more conventional moral reasoning and less post-conventional moral reasoning than do members of religious groups that encourage more flexible and abstract ways of approaching biblical material (Ernsberger and Manaster, 1981). Post-conventional moral reasoners are more likely to be agnostic than to be religiously affiliated. This of course may be a reflection of the liberal-humanistic cultural values of the climate in which Kohlberg conceived his theory.

Kohlberg's and Rest's work on moral development has been criticized, particularly on the grounds of being culturally biased and gender-biased. Neither Kohlberg's interviews nor Rest's test have scoring methods in which the particular sensitivities of women to the feelings of others score highly (Gilligan, 1982). Kohlberg's views on gender differences are particularly striking and controversial, since he concluded that women tend to get 'stuck' at a relatively early stage in moral development, when consideration for the feelings of others plays an important role in moral judgement.

Gilligan (1982) thought that such considerations could represent a higher level of moral development than was suggested by Kohlberg. Gilligan outlined the following levels and transitions for women:

Level 1: Orientation to individual survival, followed by the first transition: from selfishness to individual responsibility.
Level 2: Goodness and self-sacrifice, followed by the second transition: from goodness to truth.
Level 3: The morality of non-violence, in which women come to reject the idea of self-sacrifice as having an immoral power to hurt the self. Now, avoiding the causing of pain and avoiding the abuse of power become over-riding considerations.

Gilligan's theory does not seem to have been explored in relation to religion.

Like Kohlberg's account of moral development, Freud's theories of moral development have also been criticized for gender bias. Freud suggested that the child identified with and internalized an image of the same-sex parent. This happened as a way of resolving the very strong and conflicting feelings of early childhood. The internalized parent-image is both the foundation of the image of God, and the foundation of the conscience. The behaviour of very young children is amoral, but as social experience with caretakers is accrued, the child internalizes their behaviour and is able to anticipate reactions to his or her own behaviour, and to adjust behaviour accordingly.

The internalization of the behaviour of others, and the ability to anticipate likely reactions to our own intended behaviour and to adjust behaviour intentions, has been described by other developmental theorists as well as Freud: the symbolic interactionist G.H. Mead, for example (1934), and social learning theorists such as Bandura (1977).

It has been suggested that some types of upbringing are more likely to be associated with better moral control of behaviour. Gentle admonition, reasoning and love-withdrawal have been shown to go with stronger conscience development and moral control of behaviour than have physical punishment or power assertion (Hoffman, 1970; Brody and Shaffer, 1982).

We have already noted that internalization is fundamental both to Freudian theories of religion and morality, and to the more modern object-relations theories of religion. There have been quantified empirical studies on Freud's 'father-figure' hypothesis (chapter 5), but the main empirical work on Freudian and other hypotheses about religion has not been quantitative. They have generally involved clinical observation.

From what has been said about internalization, one would expect that conditions associated with better moral control of behaviour might also be associated with a healthier, non-authoritarian, tolerant style of religiosity. This is however speculative.

Child-rearing practices and religion

What do we know about child-rearing practices in relation to religion, and what are the effects of different types of upbringing on the religion of adulthood?

There is a little systematic evidence on both questions. There are also some interesting observations.

The best-known hypothesis is articulated by Capps (1993), put forward in an article entitled 'Religion and Child Abuse: Perfect Together'. Capps quotes a number of (Christian) sources advocating the use of corporal punishment 'for the good of the child'. For example, Fugate (1980) in 'What the Bible says about ... Child Training' advises:

> Chastisement ... should never be administered by an angry or emotional parent. If a parent cannot control himself, he should send the child to his room to wait for his whipping. This action provides the parent with time to 'cool down' and it allows the child time to ponder the coming consequences of his actions.

Capps suggested that religious sources might be encouraging the use of physical punishment of children, and that the use of physical punishment might be more likely in more religious homes.

This may not be the case. Steley (1996) interviewed a sample of 120 British adults and asked for their recall of the use of physical punishment by their parents, and their parents' religious activity. Steley's main conclusions were:

- there was no relationship between recalled parental religiosity and the use of physical punishment with children under thirteen;
- the more religious parents were less likely to use physical punishment on adolescents (over thirteen);
- when parents did use physical punishment, the more religious were less likely to use negative communication (shouting, saying damaging things), and more likely to be recalled as having a child-oriented motive;

- the more religiously active parents were recalled as having a more positive relationship with their children.

A broadly similar picture – that family relations in religious homes are reported more positively than are family relations in homes with low or zero religious activity – is drawn by Brody *et al.* (1998) for a sample of ninety African-American families in the rural South of the USA. In this study, which used observational as well as self-report methods, the higher religious activity among the parent was associated with:

- lower levels of conflict between parents;
- more cohesive family relationships;
- fewer problems among adolescent children.

Nevertheless, physical punishment has been and is used in the name of religion. Biale (1983) developed the thesis that physical punishment might have the effect of alienating youth from religion. He thought that young Jewish boys, married at a very early age, were likely to join the secular enlightenment movement if their mothers-in-law beat them. Adorno, *et al.* (1950), on the basis of their systematic study of the authoritarian personality, thought that coercive methods of child discipline were more likely to be associated with authoritarianism, and with a 'neutralized' style of religiosity.

In summary, these observations suggest that in contemporary Western society and perhaps elsewhere, religious activity may be associated with better family relationships and lower use of physical punishment. Where unpleasant, coercive styles of discipline are used in religious contexts, the effects on religious style and religious observance are likely to be negative.

Personality and religion: H.J. Eysenck's thesis

H.J. Eysenck has developed an influential theory of personality, and has extended this to make predictions about the relations between personality, religion and morality. What were these suggestions, and how far have they been supported?

Eysenck suggested that there are several fundamental dimensions of personality (e.g. Eysenck and Eysenck, 1985):

- *extraversion*, involving both sociability and impulsivity;
- *neuroticism*, or emotional instability, involving anxiety, depression, low self-esteem and tension;
- *psychoticism*, involving lack of impulse control.

Recent work on personality has identified the so-called 'Big Five' major personality factors. Although there is mild disagreement about the exact components of the Five, extraversion and neuroticism are almost always present (M.W. Eysenck, 1998). Psychoticism however is not a strong candidate for inclusion. Additionally there is uncertainty over whether it is really a factor underlying psychosis, or whether it has more to do with psychopathy ('delinquency', or anti-social behaviour). If you look at the examples of 'psychoticism' items in the box below, this last argument seems a strong one. A final problem with 'psychoticism' is that the measures of this trait do not reach the standards required of good, reliable psychological measures (Francis, Brown and Philipchalk, 1992).

A further factor on Eysenck's measures of personality is *social desirability*, assessed by the so-called *Lie scale*, which assesses the tendency of the person to give socially-desirable – 'I am a good person' – answers.

EXAMPLES FROM THE EYSENCK PERSONALITY INVENTORY AND PERSONALITY QUESTIONNAIRE

Introversion-extraversion

1. Do you mind selling things or asking people for money for good causes?
2. Do you like cracking jokes and telling funny stories to your friends?
3. Do you often get into a jam because you do things without thinking?

Neuroticism

1. Are you moody?
2. Have you often lost sleep over your worries?
3. Do you suffer from 'nerves'?

Psychoticism (low impulse control)

1. Would you take drugs which may have strange or dangerous effects?
2. Do you prefer to go your own way rather than act by the rules?
3. Do you think marriage is old-fashioned and should be done away with?

Social desirability (Lie scale)

1. As a child, did you always do as you were told immediately and without grumbling?
2. Have you sometimes told lies in your life?
3. Do you sometimes laugh at a dirty joke?

(The socially-desirable answers to the last two questions are 'no').

How might these personality factors relate to religion and morality? Eysenck invoked the concept of conditionability, the ease or readiness with which the individual becomes conditioned, learning emotional responses to particular stimuli. Punishment and admonition would be more effective with conditionable individuals. Eysenck found evidence that religious beliefs were 'tender-minded' rather than 'tough-minded'. He suggested that tender-minded attitudes arise as a result of conditioning. His chain of reasoning led to the suggestion that individuals low on extraversion – introverts – were more conditionable, and more likely to hold tender-minded attitudes, including religious and moral beliefs. Eysenck's theses about personality and religion also included the suggestions that those low on psychoticism would be more likely to hold religious beliefs, as would those high on neuroticism (Eysenck and Eysenck, 1985). Essentially:

- The more introverted will be more moral and religious because they have more conditioned prohibitions.
- Those low on P (psychoticism) will be more religious and moral because they are less impulsive.

Both these suggestions of Eysenck's – that more conditionable people, and those lower on psychoticism, would be more religious – imply a package of associations between personality, religion and morality. How far are these suggestions borne out?

Although some early research did find low associations between introversion and religiosity, and neuroticism and religiosity, this proved to be an artefact of gender. Women tend to be more introverted and more neurotic than men, and also more religious. When the associations between personality and religion are analysed separately for men and for women, the associations disappear (Brown, 1987; Francis, 1993a; Lewis and Maltby, 1995). M.W. Eysenck (1998) has pointed out that, further to these points, there is very little evidence for a general factor of conditionability, or for a relationship between ease of conditioning and attitude formation. Thus, empirically, the proposed association between religion and the personality factors introversion and neuroticism (which are supposed to underlie 'tender-mindedness' and conditionability) has not been supported.

However, low psychoticism is more strongly associated with religiosity (Lewis and Joseph, 1994). This may be the result of an underlying social desirability factor (Francis, 1992; Wilde and Joseph, 1997;

Eysenck, 1998). Most of the work on personality and religion has involved measuring religious attitudes and personality using psychometric tests, and then looking to see whether there is an association or correlation between personality and religiosity scores. These studies are very hard to interpret because it is difficult to make inferences about direction of effects. Eysenck (1998) has emphasized the need for longitudinal and experimental studies to clarify the cause-and-effect relationships. In response to Eysenck's suggestion, Lewis (1999a) has presented experimental evidence that the relations between religion and low psychoticism are not merely an artefact of social desirability. The studies that have been done could suggest a general clustering of personality and attitude factors to do with 'goodness'. Some aspects of H.J. Eysenck's theories about religion, personality and morality could still remain on the agenda for investigation.

RELIGION, STRESS AND DISTRESS

In earlier chapters, we have looked at some of the ways in which religion and well-being might be associated. Some of the effects are negative: religion, for example, might be associated with shame and guilt, which may lower well-being. But the overall associations between religion and well-being tend to be positive (Bergin, 1983; Loewenthal, 1995; Worthington *et al.*, 1996).

The general effect masks a range of specific effects. Here, three groups of effects will be focused upon (other examples appear in chapter 5):

1. Religion may affect the *quality and quantity of stress*, which in turn affects well-being and distress.
2. Religious groups offer high levels of *social support*, which can protect individuals from some of the worst effects of stress.
3. Religious-group membership involves a range of activities such as prayer, study and listening to encouraging or inspiring speeches, which may provide individuals with a range of beliefs (*cognitive resources*) which might also help to protect against some of the miserable results of stress.

How might religion affect the quality and quantity of stress? In one analysis (Loewenthal *et al.*, 1997a, 1997b, 1998) it was suggested that people living in traditional religious groups suffered more frequently from minor stressful events, compared with people who were not associated with any religious group. They had busy lives, full of obligations, many of which were directly or indirectly a result of their religious involvement. A high frequency of these minor stressors was in turn associated with a high frequency of mild anxiety. People worried a lot about keeping up with all the things they were obliged to do (see chapter 5). Mild anxiety was more prevalent among traditional religious groups, than among the non-affiliated. On the other hand, people in traditional religious groups were less likely to suffer from more serious disruptive events, such as divorce or family violence. These disruptive events were, in turn, associated with major depressive disorder.

To summarize so far, religion can affect patterns of stress, and this can affect patterns of distress and of minor psychiatric disorder. We could suggest that minor anxiety is a disorder associated with the religious life, while major depression is a disorder associated with secularization.

The second suggestion we wanted to consider was whether social support might be a feature of religious groups. Social support might help to protect from some of the effects of stress. Two contrasting examples are described in the box below.

◆

Henry was a British boy. He had married a German girl, Ilse, who had come to Britain as an au pair. They were very happy together, but Ilse did not like Britain, and Henry was willing to give Germany a try. They moved to Germany and they both found jobs. Ilse worked in business administration, which she enjoyed, and which paid well. Henry's German was not fluent, and he had no time to study since they needed both sets of wages to pay for the apartment they were buying. Henry worked as a semi-skilled builder, which he found quite tiring because he had been in a desk job before moving to Germany. Then, as a result of the heavy manual work, he suffered from a repetitive strain injury and had to give up the job. Because of his injury, and because of his poor German it was very hard to find alternative employment. He looked back to the golden days in Britain when he had a pleasant, secure, prestigious career. He did not keep his feelings a secret from Ilse, who meanwhile became angry because she was supporting a 'useless layabout parasite'. The arguments became more bitter, with Ilse telling Henry that if he thought Britain was so wonderful, he could go back to where he came from. One night, Henry did just that, having borrowed money for the fare back to London. Once there, he began job-hunting, but he had been out of employment for so long that he met with no success. His parents were sympathetic, and would have been happy for him to live at home. But he feared that it would be even harder to find work in the area where they lived. Also he felt too proud to go back to being supported and sheltered by his parents. He felt his life was a mess and that he was a useless, hopeless person.

◆

Eva, aged 62, was struggling home with several heavy bags of shopping. It was a bitterly cold day and as she struggled along she failed to notice a patch of ice. She slipped, heard a cracking noise and found she could not stand on her left leg.

It was a complicated fracture and Eva needed some time in hospital. She became very anxious about how her husband and handicapped daughter would manage. Although Eva and her husband were in their 60s, Eva's husband still ran his small business and was out of the house for long hours. Their daughter, Susan, was confined to a wheel-chair, somewhat learning-disabled, and needed round-the-clock care. She had never been able to find an appropriate job and it was very unlikely that she would ever be able to live independently.

Eva had two married sons living close by. Whilst Eva was in hospital one son and his wife took charge of Susan, who was sent to respite care during the day because the sister-in-law had young children and could not cope with a handicapped adult full-time. Susan was happy in the respite home where there were structured activities, pleasant carers, and friends to be made. Even when Eva eventually came home, Susan continued to visit the respite centre regularly, and everyone felt that the quality of both Susan's and Eva's lives had been improved by this. Whilst she was away, Eva's husband alternated between his sons' homes for dinner every evening. Sometimes he would take Susan to visit her mother in hospital, sometimes he would visit the hospital by himself. When Eva came home, she was mobile but needed help with housework, cooking, shopping and caring for Susan. Her husband, sons, daughters-in-law, many friends and neighbours rallied round, and a district nurse and a home-help also came in regularly for a few weeks. People went shopping, brought in cooked meals, took Susan to the care centre, helped with Susan in the evenings, helped with the housework, and also visited Eva to keep her company. Eva had felt anxious and somewhat despairing when she first realized how helpless she was going to be, and for how long. Although she continued to walk somewhat stiffly and with a limp, she eventually recovered almost fully, but was pleased to let Susan go to the care centre every day. She was very grateful to her relations and friends, and to the welfare and health care organizations (some of them connected with religious groups), both for the practical support, and for the company, the opportunity to talk things through, and to feel part of a family and of a community.

About one year after the accident, Eva took stock of her situation. She was not walking as well as she had done before the accident, and there had been no improvement in recent months in spite of her efforts in physiotherapy. Her big worry was of course Susan. Eva was more or less managing without any more help than she had had before the accident, except that now Susan went to the care centre every day. But the accident had made Eva realize that she was unlikely to be able to care for Susan for the rest of Susan's life. She became very low and anxious, and called in her rabbi. She told him she could not assume that her sons and daughters-in-law would be able and willing to care for Susan if 'anything happened' to her and her husband. She did not know whether Susan would adjust to living permanently in the care centre, even if there were space for her. She said she felt a return of the depression that had troubled her after Susan was born and her difficulties were first diagnosed. The depression had lifted a little in the day-to-day round of caring for the children, but had remained as a submerged set of angry questions. Why did God do this to people? What had Susan done that she should be unable to walk or to care for herself or to enjoy the pleasures that were available to people with normal intellectual functioning. She would never know the happiness of finding her partner in life, of loving a man, of having children. Eva's rabbi tried to offer her some comfort, but suggested that if she continued to feel low, she should seek professional help – perhaps a counsellor, therapist, or somebody recommended by her doctor. Or she could join a community support group, which had recently been started, for adult carers. Eva thought over these suggestions and decided that she had been living with her concerns for long enough. They had been with her since Susan was a baby, and the accident had brought it all up again. She went along to the support group and came home in tears after the first meeting. Her husband was very concerned, but Eva said that this was the first time she had ever been able to cry about Susan. She somehow felt that this crying was something she had tried to do but it had never before happened. Meeting other people with similar burdens, and meeting people who could feel for her, was something she had not experienced before, and somehow this released her weeping, pent up for so many years. She kept going to the group. After a few weeks she began to feel some hope that her situation could be borne with, and that something could be worked out for Susan's long-term future. Meanwhile she began to feel that she had a life to live, for the sake of herself, for Susan and her husband, the rest of the family and the rest of the community.

(Brown and Harris, 1978; Champion and Aris, 1988;1992)

◆

The main elements of social support are:

- people who know and care about you;
- people in whom you can confide, and with whom you can discuss your problems;
- people who can offer and give practical help.

If Henry belonged to a church, for example, he might be helped by talking to a priest or a sympathetic fellow-member. Friends might help him to find work. Some of Eva's support came or could have come from religious group membership. A number of researchers have suggested that these kinds of resources – emotional and practical social support – are more available in religious groups, and may help to buffer the effects of stress. The end result may be somewhat better mental health for members of religious groups (Prudo *et al.*, 1984; Shams and Jackson, 1993; McIntosh, *et al.*, 1993).

Thirdly, there are cognitive effects of religious-group membership. These may also have a stress-buffering function, or sometimes they may create or cause stress and distress. If Henry belonged to a church he might, for example, hear sermons or read religious texts which might strengthen his faith or trust, his belief that he should do his best and trust that God will take care of things in the way that is ultimately best for him. He could pray that God help him find a job and improve his social and emotional life (finding a more appropriate partner in life). This might help to give him a little hope. These beliefs may be associated with better mental health outcomes in people under stress.

Figure 6.1. Relations between religious activity, beliefs and outcomes in individuals under stress (based on Loewenthal, MacLeod, et al., 2000).

Religious ideas may not always be consoling. Gilbert (1992) interviewed recently bereaved parents in the USA (see box). Some found consolation – Gilbert suggested that religion might be a resource for bereaved parents. But some found religious ideas irritating, meaningless, or infuriating. Generally the latter were unlikely to be church members, while the former were.

◆

RELIGION AS A RESOURCE FOR BEREAVED PARENTS

Bereaved parents who found religious ideas helpful

'There's no doubt in my mind ... if we didn't know that God had it all under control, then things would have been a lot different. I think I would have had a real hard time.'

'I accepted that God knew there was something wrong and that's why she had died. And He knew that, whatever was wrong, we couldn't handle it, between ourselves, and that was His will.'

'God gave this to me because I could handle it more than other people.'

'They say there's reasons for God to do everything, you know. I think that's very true because I love him (the second child, born after the death of the first) a lot more now than I would have, had our first son been here.'

'It was at that time that I really got close to Him through prayer and that, and it was that summer after she died that I surrendered to the ministry.'

'I realized that I had to change my attitude towards life, that I had to forgive myself, forgive my husband and praise God that we were still all alive ... And I think I turned to God then too.'

'He said, "Who do you blame?" And I said, "Well I blame God and He caused it to happen." And he made me realize that it wasn't God's fault.'

Bereaved parents who did not find religious ideas helpful

'It was just very hard to be close to God, and I just kind of wanted to turn away, to be angry ... At the time, I felt like I wanted to be as far away from God as I could get. Do things to make him angry, that kind of thing, because I felt He had made me angry.'

'[The priest] told me I should be delighted that I had an angel in heaven ... He was worse than nothing, the man was a jackass.'

'I got "It's God's will" ... and I finally laid into one person and I said, "What possible good could come from making my wife so sick and killing my child?" And they said, "Well, you don't always understand the plan." And I said, "I'm sorry, but there is no ultimate plan to justify this," and I said, "Hitler had a plan."'

'I just remember feeling that frustration ... Some people, meaning well but doing the typical thing of coming up and telling me that it was God's will and all that stuff and I didn't want to hear it at the time.'

'I had a preacher come in when my son was dying and, oh, you would've thought! I cursed this guy, you know, because he said, "We don't always understand but I, you know, maybe with something you appreciate things more" or something. I can't remember what he said. And I, oh, I just went nuts on this guy! And I said, "Let me take you through there and show you these babies with their arms off and their guts hanging off, and if this is supposed to make me appreciate my arms more, you know, if God sent this baby here, I think He's crummy!" I don't believe that God would send a child here to make you appreciate things more.'

'[When people told me it was for the best] Really, would you like to tell me why, what's the best about it? It's for the best and someday you'll know what God's plan was for you and there's a reason for all this. Oh really! There's no reason for this stuff. You can't tell me there's a reason.'

'I don't think either one of us considers ourselves terribly religious, so that wasn't something I would fall back on. It wasn't something I would count as something that would help at that time. But then, even before, it wasn't.'

(Quoted in Gilbert, 1992)

◆

Religious explanations – saying that God was a cause of something – may be offered for some events (Furnham and Brown, 1992; Loewenthal and Cornwall, 1993). Such explanations may be offered more frequently for more major and uncontrollable events, such as life-threatening illnesses, for example. These explanations are a bit of a double-edged weapon as far as their consoling power is concerned. For example, God may be blamed for bad events, and the individual may feel angry.

Pargament *et al.* (1990) have made careful study of the features of religion associated with positive mental health outcomes following a severe negative life event. These researchers confirmed the importance of various features of coping that are not specifically religious. For example, focusing on the positive, regarding the situation as an opportunity to grow, and having social support, were all associated with positive mental health outcomes. They developed a number of scales to assess different aspects of religious coping, probably the most systematic and rigorous study of religious coping efforts and their outcomes. The scales measured the following methods of religious coping:

- spiritually-based, e.g. 'Took control over what I could, and gave the rest up to God', 'Used my faith to help me decide how to cope with the situation';

- good deeds, e.g. 'Attended religious services or participated in religious rituals', 'Led a more loving life';
- discontent, e.g. 'Felt angry with or distant from God';
- pleading, e.g. 'Asked for a miracle';
- religious avoidance, e.g. 'Prayed or read the bible to keep my mind off my problems'.

Religious aspects of coping that were associated with better mental health outcomes were:

- beliefs in a just, benevolent God;
- experience of God as a supportive partner in coping;
- involvement in religious rituals;
- search for support through religion.

Seeing one's troubles as God's punishment, however, was associated with poorer mental health outcomes, a finding that has been replicated several times (Pargament and Brant, 1998 *et al.*, Koenig *et al.* 1998).

It has been suggested that guilt and shame may be encouraged in religious groups. This may be true as far as guilt is concerned (Luyten *et al.*, 1998), but does not seem to be true for shame. It has also been asked whether religious guilt and/or shame may lower self-esteem. There is no clear evidence for this, partly because of the healing effects of forgiveness and acceptance, quite positive feelings which may often follow on from guilt or shame (Watson *et al.*, 1988a, 1988b, 1988c).

Although it has been frequently suggested that there are overall positive associations between religion and well-being, we have just seen that there are both positive and negative effects of religion on well-being.

RELIGION AND PREJUDICE

This section deals with one of the great paradoxes of the psychology of religion, in fact probably the greatest. The major religions all claim to teach the brotherhood of man and the sisterhood of women. They all claim to teach love or at least respect for fellow-humanity. *Prejudice* is used here in the sense of derogatory views of the socially unlike. Members of other groups are seen as inferior, and not as fully human as members of one's own group. They do not merit sympathy, and may be seen as repositories of bad characteristics: laziness, immorality, dishonesty, slyness, violence, stupidity, craftiness, cruelty. The classic research on prejudice, by Adorno *et al.* (1950) identified several prejudice-related traits: authoritarianism (tendency to fascism), ethnocentrism, political and economic conservatism, and anti-Semitism. All were strongly inter-related. Ethnocentrism was defined as in-group loyalty, plus distrust and dislike for members of other groups.

The great paradox is that there are generally consistent associations between measures of religious behaviour and measures of prejudice: the more religious are generally the more prejudiced (Argyle and Beit-Hallahmi, 1975; Beit-Hallahmi and Argyle, 1997; Paloutzian, 1996).

Allport's resolution

Gordon Allport tackled this paradox in a series of publications (Allport, 1950, 1959, 1966; Allport and Ross, 1967) drawing on his experience of work in the study of personality to examine the psychology of religion in general, and the religion-prejudice paradox in particular.

In doing this, Allport set himself against current thinking in the scientific establishment, where the *Zeitgeist* was very much anti-religion and anti the study of religion (see chapter 1). In 1950 Allport published *The Individual and His Religion*, a study which involved in-depth interviewing of American adults, including large numbers who had served as soldiers in World War II, and who had experienced horrors unthinkable to their contemporaries in the USA. Allport identified a large proportion of adults (about ninety per cent of his sample) who experienced a felt need for some form of religion. Most were not affiliated to organized religious groups. Many had experienced very great stress, including battle and other war experiences, and Allport was particularly interested in how individuals come to terms with such experience. In this 1950 book, he suggested a distinction between the religion of childhood, in which God is trusted to take care of the individual, to look after him or her, and their family and loved ones, and generally to take care of things nicely. This childlike trust is generally appropriate in childhood, but Allport suggested that adults still nurturing this form of religiosity in adulthood have had to turn a blind eye to the sufferings they have encountered. Allport regarded this form of religiosity as immature. Immature religious individuals may be complacent, judgemental, unsympathetic to others' distress, and self-preoccupied. The childlike trust that God will take care of things nicely, especially as they pertain to oneself and one's own group, is challenged by encounters with suffering, and this form of faith must be revised. Some possible responses are:

- How can God do this? I am angry with God.
- There is no God. If there were, things like this could not happen.
- These bad things are happening out there to others, but not to me and mine, thankfully. Maybe they did something to deserve it. We are safe. We are good people and will be OK.
- I don't understand this. It's happened and I just have to accept it. There's nothing much I can do about it.
- I don't understand this. This might be what God wants, but it's beyond me. I just have to try to roll with the punches, be grateful for the kindness of others, and do my best to feel for others who are suffering and do what I can to help them.

The last set of responses are characteristic of what Allport called a mature philosophy of life, which may not be explicitly religious. The mature individual is tolerant of others, sympathetic, not self-preoccupied, and may place great demands on themselves.

> The mature sentiment is 1) well-differentiated 2) dynamic in character in spite of its derivative nature 3) productive of a consistent morality 4) comprehensive 5) integral 6) fundamentally heuristic. It will be seen that these criteria are nothing else than special applications in the religious sphere of the test for maturity of personality: a widened range of interests, insight into oneself, and the development of an adequately embracing philosophy of life.
>
> (Allport, 1950)

Clearly the shift from immature to mature religion does not occur independently of other changes. It is a feature of overall restructuring of character, cognitive style, patterning of social relationships and existential outlook.

Allport's distinction between immature and mature (religious) philosophies or outlooks on life was to prove important in his attempts to unravel the relationships between religion and prejudice. In later publications, the 'immature-religion' concept was gradually revised and replaced by the concept of the *extrinsic* religious orientation, while the 'mature-religion' concept was revised and replaced by the concept of the *intrinsic* religious orientation.

LIVERPOOL JOHN MOORES UNIVERSITY
LEARNING SERVICES

Extrinsic orientation: persons with this orientation are disposed to use religion for their own ends ... extrinsic values are always instrumental and utilitarian. Persons with this orientation may find religion useful in a variety of ways – to provide security and solace, sociability and distraction, status and self-justification. The embraced creed is lightly held or else selectively shaped to fit more primary needs. In theological terms the extrinsic type turns to God, but without turning away from self.

Intrinsic orientation: persons with this orientation find their master motive in religion. Other needs, strong as they may be, are regarded as of less ultimate significance, and they are, so far as possible, brought into harmony with the religious beliefs and prescriptions. Having embraced a creed the individual endeavours to internalise it and follow it fully. It is in this sense that he *lives* his religion.

(Allport and Ross, 1967)

You can probably guess the outlines of Allport's suggestions about religion and prejudice from what has been said so far. Extrinsically oriented individuals are said to use their religion for self-serving ends, and are unlikely to lose any sleep over finding features of humanity in the culturally unlike, since the embraced creed is 'lightly held'. Thus Allport would predict an overall association between prejudice and extrinsic religion. Conversely the intrinsically oriented individual tries to follow the embraced creed fully, and other needs including selfish ones are brought into subservience. Allport suggested an inverse relationship between prejudice and intrinsic religion. As for the overall empirically found association between prejudice and religion, Allport accounted for this by proposing a preponderance of extrinsic religiosity, or of extrinsically religious individuals. Very highly religiously active individuals are lower in prejudice than moderately religious, and the suggestion is that these are more likely to be religiously intrinsic.

These suggestions were tested empirically (Allport and Ross, 1967). It is important to bear in mind that extrinsic and intrinsic religious orientations are not actually distinct 'types', in spite of Allport and Ross's use of the term 'type'. In the Allport and Ross study, the two dimensions did not correlate: it was equally possible to be high on both, low on both, or high on one and low on the other. A slightly simplified view of the main findings is outlined in Table 6.1.

Table 6.1   Prejudice and religious orientation (based on Allport and Ross, 1967)

	High extrinsic	Low extrinsic
High intrinsic	High prejudice	Low prejudice
Low intrinsic	High prejudice	Low prejudice

The important points in Table 6.1 are that although the high-E low-I person is high on prejudice, and the low-E high-I is low on prejudice, as Allport suggested, the highest levels of prejudice were shown by those who were high on both extrinsic *and intrinsic*. Allport called these indiscriminately pro-religious, mindlessly enthusiastic about any proposition to do with religion.

Batson *et al.* (1993) offer their readers an impressive overview of research on orientations to religion. One of their suggestions is to invite readers to read through items from the intrinsic and extrinsic scales of religious orientation used by Allport and Ross (see box).

——————————————————— ◆ ———————————————————

ITEMS ON THE EXTRINSIC AND INTRINSIC ORIENTATION SCALES

Extrinsic scale
1. Although I believe in my religion, I feel there are many more important things in my life.
2. It doesn't matter so much what I believe so long as I lead a moral life.
3. The primary purpose of prayer is to gain relief and protection.
4. The church is most important as a place to formulate good social relationships.
5. What religion offers me most is comfort when sorrow and misfortune strike.
6. I pray chiefly because I have been taught to pray.
7. Although I am a religious person I refuse to let religious considerations influence my everyday affairs.
8. A primary reason for my interest in religion is that my church is a congenial social activity.
9. Occasionally I find it necessary to compromise my religious beliefs in order to protect my social and economic well-being.
10. One reason for my being a church member is that such membership helps to establish a person in the community.
11. The purpose of prayer is to secure a happy and peaceful life.

Intrinsic scale

1. It is important for me to spend periods of time in private religious thought and meditation.
2. If not prevented by unavoidable circumstances, I attend church.
3. I try hard to carry my religion over into all my other dealings in life.
4. The prayers I say when I am alone carry as much meaning and personal emotion as those said by me during services.
5. Quite often I have been keenly aware of the presence of God or the Divine Being.
6. I read literature about my faith (or church).
7. If I were to join a church group I would prefer to join a Bible study group rather than a social fellowship.
8. My religious beliefs are what really lie behind my whole approach to life.
9. My religion is especially important to me because it answers many questions about the meaning of life.

(Allport and Ross, 1967; this version adapted from Batson *et al.*, 1993)

◆

Batson *et al.* suggest that the intrinsic scale may not be assessing mature religion so much as a variety of fanaticism, as in Hoffer's concept of the true believer, who 'is ready to sacrifice his life for the holy cause ... whose sense of security is derived from his passionate attachment and not from the excellence of his cause' (Hoffer, 1951). Batson *et al.* find that there is substantial evidence to support the idea that many intrinsic items are associated with a tendency to see the world in terms of absolute, rigid categories. A related problem is that the tendency to agree with intrinsic religiosity items could be the result of *social desirability* factors. It simply sounds and feels good to come over as a sincere person whose religious beliefs lie behind their whole approach to life, or to describe oneself as a thoughtful and sincere person who would prefer to join a study rather than a social group. Batson, *et al.* (1978), and Watson *et al.* (1986) in fact found that intrinsic and social desirability measures were correlated, though this has not always been shown (Cooper-Green, 1998).

Hunt and King (1971) reviewed the status of the extrinsic and intrinsic concepts after several years of vigorous research activity, and concluded that although extrinsic religiosity was well operationalized and clearly conceptualized as an instrumental approach to religion, both the definition and measurement of intrinsic religiosity remained fuzzy.

Batson

Batson (1976) thought that items assessing intrinsic religiosity might be picking up fanatics, naive enthusiasts, the rigid acceptors of doctrine, and people who wished to appear in a good light, rather than genuinely open-minded, tolerant or mature personalities. Batson thought that important features of Allport's original concept of religious maturity needed to be re-incorporated into the measurement of religiosity. These features included:

- readiness to face complex problems;
- readiness to doubt and to be self-critical;
- an emphasis on incompleteness, since mature religion involves a continual search.

Batson and his colleagues have developed a number of measures of individual religion, in which features of Allport's original distinction between mature and immature religion have been sharpened:

- *Quest* assesses complexity, doubt and tentativeness in individual religion.
- *Means* (formerly extrinsic) assesses religion as a means to other, self-serving ends.
- *End* (formerly intrinsic) assesses religion as an ultimate end in itself.
- *External* assesses the extent to which an individual's external social environment has influenced (or is said to have influenced) his or her personal religion.
- *Internal* assesses the extent to which individual religion is a result of internal needs for certainty, strength and direction.
- *Orthodoxy* assesses extent of belief in traditional Christian religious doctrines.

The box on p. 138 shows some examples of items from some of these scales. One difficult feature of these measures is the understanding given by Batson *et al.* of the external measure. They say that this is a component of the extrinsic, means dimension, and that they 'assumed that religion that was a response to social influence would reflect an extrinsic, means orientation because it would presumably be motivated by a desire to gain the self-serving end of social approval'. The difficulty with this assumption is that *all* religious ideas are ultimately derived from external sources (even though they may be worked on and modified in the course of making them one's own). What the external scale is assessing is not how much people differ in the extent to which their ideas are derived from external sources, but the extent to which people *recognize* or *perceive* that their religious development has been socially influenced. Arguably, this has little to do with a desire for social approval.

◆

EXAMPLES OF ITEMS FROM THE EXTERNAL, INTERNAL AND QUEST SCALES

External (means)

1. The church has been very important for my religious development.
2. My religion serves to satisfy my needs for fellowship and security.
3. Certain people have served as models for my religious development.

Internal (end)

1. It is necessary for me to have a religious belief.
2. When it comes to religious questions, I feel driven to know the truth.
3. I find it impossible to conceive of myself not being religious.

Quest

1. As I grow and change, I expect my religion to grow and change.
2. For me, doubting is an important part of what it means to be religious.
3. There are many religious issues on which my views are still changing.

(Batson *et al.*, 1993)

◆

How do these various aspects of religiosity relate to other aspects of behaviour and thinking? By and large (Batson *et al.*, 1993):

- Extrinsic and means religion tend to be associated with *prejudice*, and with poorer mental health.
- Intrinsic, end religiosity has been associated with some indices of good mental health, and with reported religious and mystical experience. There is no, or negative, relation with prejudice. However, covert measures of prejudice show less clear relations with intrinsic religiosity.
- Quest has been associated with measures of cognitive complexity, and also helpfulness. There is weak negative relation with prejudice.

Other explorations of Batson's typology include Falbo and Shepperd's (1986) study of self-righteousness. Falbo and Shepperd developed a typology of self-righteousness by grouping all their research participants (who all had at least a moderate degree of religiosity) into four groups, according to their level of self-righteousness and self-esteem. The four groups were:

- *The broad-minded*: these were low in self-righteousness and high in self-esteem.
- *The insecure*: these were high in self-righteousness and low in self-esteem.
- *The arrogant*: these were high in both self-righteousness and in self-esteem.
- *The meek*: these were low in both self-righteousness and self-esteem.

The insecure and the arrogant had higher scores on extrinsic religiosity than the other participants. In other words, self-righteousness went along with extrinsic religiosity. The broad-minded and the meek were higher than the others on both intrinsic religiosity and quest religiosity. So low self-righteousness went along with intrinsic and quest religiosity. This study therefore offers good support for both Allport's and Batson's suggestions about religion and personality.

More recently, interest in religious orientation has begun to shift to features of cognitive style and identity. Intrinsic-ness is characterized by firm views on religiously endorsed ethical and religious issues *and* by a strong sense of identity (Watson *et al.*, 1998; Cooper-Green, 1998).

Allport's approach has been helpful in understanding some of the ways in which personal religious style relates to other features of behaviour and thinking. Allport suggested that religion 'both makes and unmakes prejudice', and we turn now to look at a further perspective on how religion makes prejudice.

Social Identity Theory

Developed by Tajfel and Turner (Tajfel, 1970, 1978; Turner, 1987; Tajfel and Turner, 1986), Social Identity Theory deals with how people as members of a social group, tend to see themselves as better and more right than members of other groups: in-group favouritism. Social Identity theorists offer important perspectives on religion and prejudice, since religious groups are of course social groups. They start with the familiar idea that we are proud of the group we belong to. And this pride relates to an aspect of our identity – our social identity. Non-members of our group, who do not share our identity, may be despised. Hewstone *et al.* (1993) for example, have explored ways in which religious identity is important in evaluating other groups, along with other factors, notably ethnic identity, language and self-esteem.

Identity theory has both pleasant and unpleasant implications in the context of religion. To start with some of the less pleasant implications, consider what happens to explanations of people's behaviour. We understand and explain behaviour very differently when 'we' and members of our group do it, than when 'they' do it – especially if 'they' are threatening to us.

Notable examples occur in the rhetoric of liberation and terrorism. We, and our group, and those we sympathize with, are fighting for basic human rights, for an end to suffering. We are ready to sacrifice ourselves (and others) to achieve this noble end. We wish to throw off the yoke of the oppressor, and we are justified in using any means to do this. They, and their group, and those who threaten us, are a bunch of inhuman, heartless monsters, without a spark of human feeling and decency. They are ready to torture and murder innocent and helpless victims.

For many years, social psychologists have been interested in the *fundamental attribution error* – the tendency to justify one's own behaviour and to condemn others. This is done by producing 'external' attributions for socially undesirable behaviour by ourselves. They are oppressing us and not allowing us to live in our country and practise our religion in freedom, and that is why we are fighting for our freedom. 'Internal' attributions are made for undesirable behaviour by others. They are a bunch of inhuman, heartless monsters, without a spark of human feeling and decency. That is why they commit these atrocities. This bias applies to people in groups, as we can see from the liberation/terrorist rhetoric. Pettigrew (1979) called this the 'ultimate attribution error', and showed that it applied at least as much to people in religious groups as to people in other kinds of groups.

More recently, Hunter, *et al.* (1991) carried out a similar demonstration to Pettigrew's. They studied Catholics and Protestants in Northern Ireland, where both groups are in a state of conflict, perceiving each other as threatening to their own group's well-being and security. Cairns

(1982) has argued that religious identity (Protestant vs. Catholic) is the most salient of social identities in Northern Ireland, over-riding the importance of gender and class for example. By the age of eleven, children can identify out-group and own-group members, using first name and other cues, and the Northern Ireland conflict is dominated by the 'never-ending struggle to achieve positive social identity. The search for positive distinctiveness emphasizes group differences without mutual respect. Damage to the out-group may enhance positive psychological distinctiveness.' In the study by Hunter *et al.*, the research participants watched several clips of newsreel footage, showing various significant events in the Northern Ireland conflict. Included was a clip of a Protestant attacking Catholic mourners at a funeral using hand grenades and an automatic pistol, and another clip showing a group of Catholics attacking a car containing two soldiers (British, symbolically and politically aligned with the Protestant cause), using a variety of improvised weapons. The soldiers were in an unmarked car, and were out of uniform. They were dragged from the car and taken away, stripped, scalped and shot through the back of the head (Lewis, 1999b).

The analyses by Hunter *et al.* of Protestant and Catholic subjects' explanations of these behaviours were in line with Pettigrew's predictions about the 'ultimate attribution error'. Violence by one's own group is defensible, more likely to be seen as externally than internally caused: it is provoked. Violence by the other group is indefensible, more likely to be seen as internally than externally caused: it is unprovoked by the innocent victims, and the result of the perpetrators 'psychopathy' or 'bloodlust'.

Cognitive processes of the kind described by Pettigrew and others play an important part – not just in maintaining conflict, but in making the situation worse. So many conflicts involve confrontations across the lines of religious affiliation, and the cognitive biases involved in justification may be implicated in prejudice and cruelty. Fuller analysis of cognitive biases and their implications can be found in Brewin (1988), and of cruelty and malice in Berke (1990). Here, we have concentrated on how religious groups, by virtue of being groups, may be implicated in prejudice and cruelty.

Before leaving this unpleasant but very important topic, one further very important cognitive bias should be described: the 'just world' belief. This is *the tendency to blame victims of misfortune for their own fate*, to believe that the deformed, the poor, the afflicted are in some way *inferior*, and this perceived inferiority is both a cause and a result of the person's suffering. Lerner (1980) has suggested that the belief in a 'just world' makes us all mini-persecutors and accomplices in persecution. A suffering person is actually seen as inferior, bad, and somehow deserving of their fate, simply because they are suffering. When I describe one of Lerner's early experiments in lectures, there are looks of incredulity and disbelief – and then the protests: of course *we* wouldn't think like that! Lerner (1991) has suggested that we do have a hypocritical ability to operate on two levels: to make horrible judgements about other people who are suffering, and to deny that we are capable of making such judgements. Lerner's experiment was on a class of psychology students. They were all going to get credits for taking part in an experiment, in which one volunteer member of the class would learn something. The volunteer would receive electric shocks, however, every time they made an error in their learning. The rest of the class would fill in ratings of the learner and her performance. A nice girl volunteered to be the learner, and was seen to suffer quite considerably. Were the others grateful? If so, they had an odd way of showing it, because their ratings of the girl showed they didn't think much of her.

Lerner and his colleagues have carried versions of this experiment with all kinds of controls and comparisons, and the effect is a fairly robust one. Lerner said that no one would believe it, though basically all show evidence of this type of thinking. The suffering person is generally seen as inferior to the comfortable rest of the world, for reasons outlined above. It is suggested that this belief is fostered and/or exacerbated by religious views on sin and punishment. A suffering person must be bad, otherwise they wouldn't be suffering. An alternative view is that just-world beliefs are endemic to human nature, a built-in cognitive bias, or a culturally-carried belief, which is expressed in religion but which is not *caused* by religion. Every now and then, the media give attention to the views of someone who is both in a prominent public position and who is a religious 'fundamentalist'. Do you remember the furore in the media caused by the police inspector who said he thought that AIDS victims deserved their fate, or by the sports personality who thought that handicapped people might have committed a sin in a previous incarnation? Atkinson (1993) thought that such religiously-based attitudes were endemic, and led to inertia in dealing with those suffering from illness. It is all very well for sober religious authorities like Maimonides (1967) to propose that the politically- (or rather religiously-) correct posture is to think that one's own suffering might indicate the need to improve, but one is forbidden to be judgemental about the sufferings of others. With another's suffering, the appropriate response *ought* normally be to look for ways to help. But the just-world belief can lead to judgementalism, inertia and condemnation.

Thus the just-world belief can lead to indifference to the sufferings of others, the belief that their fate is deserved. These are features of prejudice, and we have seen that there are arguments that religion may foster the just-world belief, other arguments that the 'just world' belief is independent of religion, and other arguments that the 'just world' belief is prohibited by religion.

What is the case, empirically? I concluded (Loewenthal, 1997) that the relations between religion and beliefs about illness and suffering varied with the type of misfortune and with the type of religious background and orientation. Furnham and Brown (1992) collected explanations for suffering from interviews, and found that 'theological' explanations were indeed more likely to be endorsed by religious than by irreligious people, and also by Muslims and Jews rather than by Catholics and Protestants. These theological explanations did include a belief in divine punishment. The theological explanations for suffering were:

- that good may come from evil;
- it shows the reality of evil;
- it is a punishment sent from God;
- it is part of God's plan;
- it tests our faith in God.

However Furnham and Brown were looking at beliefs about hypothetical disasters. In a more grounded study of psychiatric nurses, Lederach and Lederach (1987) looked at the relations between religiosity and beliefs about the causes and cures of mental illness. In this study, the nurses from more religious backgrounds were not more likely to see mental illness as caused by God. However, they were more likely than the less religious nurses to consider divine intervention as potentially important in the healing process. A major review by Furnham and Procter (1989) reported conflicting relationships between measures of religiosity and a measure of just-world beliefs, the Rubin and Peplau (1973, 1975) BJW – Belief in a Just World measure. Some reports showed a positive relationship, while others showed a negative relationship. However, members of religious

LIVERPOOL
JOHN MOORES UNIVERSITY
AVRIL ROBARTS LRC
TITHEBARN STREET
LIVERPOOL L2 2ER
TEL. 0151 231 4022

groups with more structured belief systems, such as Catholics and Jews, tended to score higher on BJW. There were other relationships between BJW and a range of socio-demographic and attitude measures, although Furnham and Procter were rather critical of the worth of the BJW. They quoted Lerner (1980) who thought that the BJW tapped a 'very naive' view of social reality. Furnham and Procter also thought that there was scope to explore the relations between religious orientation and BJW, presumably with the starting hypothesis that BJW might relate positively to extrinsic religiosity, and negatively with intrinsic and/or quest religiosity. This remains to be investigated.

The belief in a just world is clearly an unpleasant but prevalent cognitive bias, which is not making the world a better place. Does religion play a role in fostering such beliefs? The findings are complicated and mixed, but it is likely that a dogmatic style of religiosity may be associated with belief in a just world.

RELIGION AND IDENTITY

We previously looked at whether and how religious group membership might be implicated in prejudice. A more positive aspect of group membership is the sense of membership and belonging one gets from belonging to a group. This sense of belonging develops almost immediately after the group is formed, or after the group is joined. New members may wish to prove themselves by enthusiastic displays of adherence to favoured group norms. Codol (1975) described this as 'the superior conformity of the self'. Not only may there be superior conformity, but perceived superior conformity: the new member sees themselves as performing much better than the old hands. New members of religious groups may distinguish themselves by keen adherence to every detail of dress and behaviour that they discover to be important (Spero, 1987). Newly-enthused 'old' members may also behave in this way. Revivalist and fundamentalist movements may involve group displays of superior conformity.

Idler (1995) offered another suggestion about the development of religious identity – bodily suffering may heighten spiritual awareness. Idler interviewed a sample of disabled clients from a rehabilitation clinic. The participants in this research 'provide insight into the meaning of identities based on spiritual or religious criteria' (see box opposite).

PHYSICAL DISABILITY MAY ENHANCE RELIGIOUS AWARENESS AND IDENTITY

There are accounts from respondents who felt that help from God or their religion changed everything in their lives. Perhaps the most dramatic stories were of religious awakenings that took place directly as a result of sudden illness or injury.

'I don't know ... I felt so spiritual, you know [after the stroke]. It was such a – you know – beautiful experience. I get like that every now and then ... I got this relaxed feeling and feel so good. I don't think you could feel that good all the time. We couldn't walk around feeling like that daily. One thing, I stopped worrying as much as I used to, and I have been able to let go of certain things that I couldn't let go of before. And, you know, I used to sit and cry because I was so happy ... it's a great way to feel ... I learned to be by myself. I get lonely sometimes, but I can deal with it more now. So in a sense I look at my stroke as a blessing ... through this stroke I started to feel more spiritual.'

These are the words of a fifty-one-year-old black Protestant woman who had been a typist before her stroke. She is still partially paralysed, and speaks elsewhere of looking down at her hands, which she cannot move. Rather than regret her loss of skill and ability to earn a living, she thinks of those who have had a stroke and who have not survived. She says she feels fortunate to be alive, and says that her life has been enriched by the experience.

Another woman who saw her illness as a turning point was a thirty-five-year-old black Protestant woman, who had also had a stroke. 'At the time before my stroke, I had no experience with my God. With my stroke I learned from him. It happened with faith. My pastor and my friends talked to me about religion. I was not very serious about religion. [Now] I take God seriously, deeply. People in my church pray for me and visit me all the time. They call me and give me support.'

Both these women had some connection before their illness. As one man explained: 'When your life drastically changes I think if you had any religious training or background you tend to resort or turn to it, or think of it, or find it more enhancing or helpful. Due to my injury, I've become more religious.' This man was a fifty-two-year-old white Protestant fabric designer. He was paralysed after a mugging in which he was stabbed in the back.

(Quoted in Idler, 1995)

Idler thought that these respondents saw a growth in their spiritual lives, an enhancement and development of their religious identity, which was given greater salience, as 'a direct result of their shrinking physical capacity'.

Members of minority groups may also be particularly dependent upon religious group membership for self-esteem, social support and satisfaction. Thus Jacobson (1997) has suggested that for young Pakistanis in Britain, religious identity is an important source of self-esteem. In Jacobson's study, young Pakistanis were reported to make a sharp distinction between religion and culture. They saw many customs as coming from culture, and not from religion. Customs which are seen as carried by culture are not seen as obligatory:

> "Most things we tend to do are culture, rather than the religion. Religion is five times a day prayer, being good, whereas culture is getting married in red, and arranged marriages. So I got married in shocking pink!"

> "Culture is a way of living in a society. Religion is living on your own. You understand? Our culture it's like – if you have a wedding, a religious wedding would be – there'd be a little bit of music, just that, but in our culture, it's getting away from religion – they have a henna night when they do it to the girl [put henna on her], they have an oil night, when they put oil in her hair – that's [just] culture, that's custom. That's getting away from religion."

Jacobson's research participants had a derogatory view of 'culture', unlike their view of religion (Islam). The former has only local relevance, to Pakistan, while the latter has universal relevance. Culture and ethnicity have permeable boundaries. Religion offers clear-cut social boundaries.

> "How would I describe Pakistani culture? Um – a touch of Islam, Hindu and Sikh culture and tradition, with a bit of the British Empire somewhere in there. Something like this. It's something to do with them three."

> "[Pakistani culture] is very backward. I mean, basically because they don't follow Islam. That's what our culture's about, yeah. And they manipulate tradition. If they were to follow Islam, it would be pretty good, but they don't. Just tradition."

> "Islam is much more easily accessible than it is back home, because of a lot of cultural influences that are totally wrong. And so practising Islam is a lot easier here. Like if I went back in hijab (head-covering worn by women), I'd have all sorts of stick from my family."

Religion thus becomes a positive and primary source of identity:

"[I would identify myself] hopefully as a Muslim! That's how I'd like to be recognized. Not as a Pakistani, or a British person or anything. As a Muslim."

"[I would describe my identity as] Muslim. And a Pakistani. But somebody in England. No I wouldn't say that! I'd just say that I'm a Muslim, and it doesn't really matter what country. At the end of the day, it's really religion, don't you reckon?"

"I'm a Muslim first. That should be promoted first. That's what's important, not the fact where you're from. Because that also creates divisions, you see. Because when you start promoting your own countries, that's when people will start thinking, oh we're better, because we're from Pakistan."

These young people saw ethnic identity as a source of conflict and divisiveness. Paradoxically, they saw their religious identity as overcoming this divisiveness. Their talk shows clearly how religious group membership can be the most salient source of social identity. This can be true for other minority groups as well (Griffith and Bility, 1996; Loewenthal and Cinnirella, 1999b).

In Griffith and Bility's study of Black Christianity, it is argued that 'in return for substantive allegiance to the group, members are often provided with food, shelter, clothing, security, a social structure, *a sharper sense of identity* (my emphasis) and a simple but coherent belief system. Social welfare and economic self-help are common aspects of black groups. All this is shrouded in the mystery of the group's rituals and an intense emotional appeal that is sometimes incomprehensible to outsiders.' In Griffith and Bility's account of Father Divine's movement, branches of the movement were called Kingdoms. Members gave up existing family ties to be reborn into the Kingdoms. Their new social identity was affirmed by their status as angels. Each angel's name was received by revelation: Crystal Star, Job Patience, Faithful Mary. These names 'represented a conscious separation of the individual from the non-group community' – and their connection to their new life and identity.

Ganzevoort (1998a, 1998b) has emphasized the importance of religious identity in coping. Based on Pargament's formulation, Ganzevoort suggests that there are four central dimensions involved in religious coping:

- crisis and coping;
- religion;
- identity;
- context.

To illustrate this, here is a case presented by Ganzevoort.

Berend was born in the early 1960s to an upper middle-class family. Both his parents are well educated. His first seven years he remembers as warm and harmonious, but the relationships in his family were not close. As the family became better off financially, they moved to an expensive house in a new neighbourhood. Now they were thrust upon each other and the atmosphere became more tense. His parents began arguing regularly, and these arguments became physically violent. Berend sided with his mother, and also tried to mediate. When he was seventeen, Berend's parents divorced, and Berend failed his end of year exams. He also experienced sexual and medical problems. After completing school, he spent a year simply living in a depressed state. He then spent several years travelling and trying various courses of study. Finally he started working in a museum. Ever since he was a young boy, Berend had been interested in questions of meaning and religion. His grandmother was important in this respect. To Berend, she symbolized a spiritual life. Like his grandmother, he joined a liberal Mennonite church. When aged twenty-five, a friend invited him to a Pentecostal service, and Berend was impressed when he saw a woman being cured through prayer. Because of his own medical problems and his wish for a solution, Berend joined this church and remained with this congregation for several years.

Eventually, however, Berend discovered several aspects of the group's doctrines with which he did not agree. Moreover, none of his medical or other problems were resolved. He then joined a commune which offered lodging and counselling for young people in distress. Berend became a counsellor. However, his own problems failed to resolve, and he left. He is planning to take up a new area of study. He has undergone counselling himself, and also surgery, but is still awaiting relief.

(Described in Ganzevoort, 1998a)

Ganzevoort comments that Berend is a seeker rather than a believer, that he has difficulty in finding religious meaning in life, and in giving meaning to his history: he lives with a fragmented self. Ganzevoort argues that narrative is important in religious coping; in Pargament's term, his narrative shows a search for significance in ways relating to the sacred. Individual identity and social context are 'visibly important in the process'.

Finally, we turn from identity in relation to the coping process, and take a last look at identity in relation to prejudice. In looking at the effects of group membership on attributions and explanations of behaviour, we considered the suggestion that group membership can enhance some of the kinds of thinking that are associated with prejudice, inter-group conflict in general, warfare, and cruelty. We now have to consider a suggestion which seems paradoxical. It has been suggested (for example by Watson *et al.*, 1998) that intrinsic religiosity is associated with a strong sense of identity, and this explains why intrinsics may adhere so strongly to approved beliefs, such as tolerance, respect and love for other people. It is worth noting that Watson *et al.* used an identity measure based on Erikson (see chapter 3), rather than one based on social identity theory. Given that extrinsic religiosity is not associated with identity measures, and is associated with measures of prejudice, it certainly looks as if there is more work needed to understand Allport's claim that religion both makes and unmakes prejudice. The orientations to religion approach has been helpful to a point, but when we consider the findings of this approach, in relations to the implications and findings derived from identity theories, there are some paradoxes. One puzzle is the problem that extrinsics are supposed to be religious because this gives a sense of security and group belonging – but extrinsic-ness does not relate to identity achievement measures. Another puzzle is that group identity may give rise to the ultimate attribution error, a cognitive bias associated with prejudice – while religious intrinsic-ness is associated both with a strong sense of identity and a strong adherence to approved unprejudiced beliefs. Hopefully these puzzles can be resolved by continued closer examination and more precise measurement of prejudice and identity.

SUMMARY

This chapter looked at some of the ways in which religion can impact on behaviour, thought and feeling in general. We looked first at morality and how it develops, and the question of how it relates to religion. The questions were examined whether and how religion affects child-rearing practices, and how these practices in turn might affect personality and morality.

The chapter also examined ways in which religion can affect levels and types of stress, and ways in which religion might moderate the effects of stress. The relations between religion and prejudice were examined, focusing particularly on the paradoxical but important idea that religion both 'makes and unmakes prejudice'. Finally, we turned to some generally more positive aspects of religion in relation to identity.

7 CONCLUSION

This book started by saying that psychology and religion had an uneasy relationship. Is this relationship improving?

The answer is a qualified yes. Psychology had certainly served as a tool of a move to secularization, as a means to explain-away religion. The current situation looks very much as if psychology has decided that religion is here to stay, and that it is an important feature of human activity.

This book looked at the range of religious behaviours, thoughts and feelings, and at some of the influences of religion on other 'non-religious' areas of behaviour, thought and feeling. I attempted to include work on non-Christian religions, so as to avoid the accusation that the psychology of religion is only about the psychology of Christianity.

Rather than repeat the conclusions reached at the end of each chapter, I would like to take an overview and pick out some key features and trends in the psychology of religion. This selection is obviously a personal one. I will focus on three areas in which I think the psychology of religion has important applications:

1) In dealing with *mental health* problems, psychiatrists, psychologists, nurses, social workers and community welfare workers have a real need for information about religion. What are the practices and beliefs favoured by different religious groups? What is considered 'normal' behaviour within the group? How might normative behaviours and beliefs be seen by someone from outside the group? Might they be seen as psychologically disturbed? What about behaviours – like prayer – which are seen as helpful and consoling for people

under stress? When and how can we reach a consensus on religious group behaviours that really are dangerous and harmful? A great deal more work can be done to enable professionals to understand how and why religious behaviours are used, and what their effects are. Both information and research are needed, to enable better understanding, better liaison, and better practice among mental health professionals dealing with their clients, and with the families and communities of their clients.

2) *Inter-group relations.* This book looks at the question of how religious groups can be implicated in prejudice, intolerance and worse. Religious reasons may be produced as justifications for warfare and persecution. Genocide almost always involves religious issues, and is promoted as holy warfare. Dozens of sites in the world are currently or have recently been implicated, involving many millions of deaths, and the utmost barbarity. As I write, varied atrocities in Kosovo, and nail-bombs in London, fill the news headlines, while many other examples fail to catch media attention. The first urgent question for psychology is, whether there are methods *specific to religious groups* which are used to promote inter-group hostility. These need to be understood, if this problem – one of the most horrific and widespread in the human situation – is to be dealt with. The second question is how religious groups can be used as vehicles for promoting better inter-group relations. This book has shown that religion may indeed help to promote tolerance, compassion and humane values among individuals. Can more be done to use religious groups to promote the teaching and valuing of these behaviours and ideas as group norms?

3) *Interpersonal relationships.* Conflict and interpersonal violence, emotional, physical and sexual abuse, are all features of human life from which we would all hope to be free. There is scope for the psychology in promoting a better understanding of the roles played by religion, both in endorsing or justifying these behaviours, and in helping to reduce them, and to improve compassionate and helpful interpersonal behaviour.

One response to all this might be to ask why we need psychology for all this to happen. People need to listen to each other, to understand each other, not to be violent or abusive, to respect and behave well to each other – and then the world will be a better place. All these things are endorsed and taught by religion and enforced by law. How will psychology help?

Psychology, as the study and understanding of what people *actually* do, think and feel, can help by showing where we are going wrong, and where we are not living up to the ideals that we might like to think we are. We are not doing as well as we could, and anything that helps to show how we might do better is to be welcomed.

BIBLIOGRAPHY

The Hutchinson Encyclopaedia. 1994, Oxford: Helicon Publishing.

Adorno, T.W., Frenkel-Brunswik, E., Levinson, D.J. and Sanford, R.N. 1950, *The Authoritarian Personality,* New York: Harper.

Allport, G.W., 1950, *The Individual and His Religion: A Psychological Interpretation,* New York: MacMillan.

Allport, G.W., 1959 'Religion and prejudice', *Crane Review,* 2, 1–10.

Allport, G.W., 1966, 'The religious context of prejudice', *Journal for the Scientific Study of Religion,* 5, 448–451.

Allport, G.W. and Ross, J.M., 1967 'Personal religious orientation and prejudice', *Journal of Personality and Social Psychology,* 5, 432–443.

Argyle, M., 1958, *Religious Behaviour,* London: Routledge & Kegan Paul.

Argyle, M. and Beit-Hallahmi, B., 1975, *The Social Psychology of Religion,* London: Routledge & Kegan Paul.

Asch, S.E., 1955, 'Opinions and social pressure' *Scientific American,* 193, 31–35.

Atkinson, J.M., 1993, 'The patient as sufferer' *British Journal of Medical Psychology,* 66, 113–120.

Bainbridge, W.S., 1997, *The Sociology of Religious Movements,* New York and London: Routledge.

Ball, H., 1987, *Why British Women Embrace Islam,* Leicester: Muslim Youth Education Council.

Bandura, A., 1977, *Social Learning Theory,* Englewood Cliffs, New Jersey: Prentice Hall.

Barker, E., 1984, *The Making of a Moonie: Choice or Brainwashing?* Oxford: Blackwell.

Barker, E., 1996 'New Religions and Mental Health', in D. Bhugra (ed.) *Psychiatry and Religion: Context, Consensus, and Controversies*, London: Routledge.

Barlow, S.H. and Bergin, A.E., 1998, 'Religion and mental health from the Mormon perspective', in H. G. Koenig (ed.) *Handbook of Religion and Mental Health*, New York: Academic Press.

Barnes, M., Doyle, D. and Johnson, B., 1989, 'The formation of a Fowler scale: An empirical assessment among Catholics', *Review of Religious Research*, 30, 412–420.

Bartholomew, K., 1997, 'Adult attachment processes: Individual and couple perspectives', *British Journal of Medical Psychology*, 70, 249–264.

Batson, C.D., 1976, 'Religion as prosocial: Agent or double agent?', *Journal for the Scientific Study of Religion*, 15, 29–45.

Batson, C.D., Naifeh, S. J. and Pate, S., 1978, 'Social desirability, religious orientation, and racial prejudice', *Journal for the Scientific Study of Religion*, 17, 31–41.

Batson, C.D., Schoenrade, P.A. and Ventis, W.L., 1993, *Religion and the Individual: A Social-Psychological Perspective*, Oxford: Oxford University Press.

Beardsworth, T., 1977, *A Sense of Presence,* Oxford: Alister Hardy Research Centre (Manchester College, now Westminster College, Oxford).

Beit-Hallahmi, B., 1989, *Prolegomena to the Psychological Study of Religion*, Cranbury, New Jersey, London, England, and Ontario, Canada: Associated University Presses.

Beit-Hallahmi, B. and Argyle, M., 1997, *The Psychology of Religious Behaviour, Belief and Experience*, London and New York: Routledge.

Belgum, D., 1992, 'Guilt and/or self-esteem as consequences of religion', *Journal of Religion and Health*, 31, 73–85.

Berger, P. and Luckman, T., 1966, *The Social Construction of Reality*, Garden City: Doubleday.

Bergin, A.E., 1983, 'Religiosity and mental health: a critical re-evaluation and meta-analysis', *Professional Psychology: Research and Practice*, 14, 170–184.

Berke, J., 1990, *The Tyranny of Malice: Explaining the Dark Side of Character and Culture*, New York: Summit Books.

Bettelheim, B., 1983, *Freud and Man's Soul*, London: Chatto & Windus.

Bhugra, D., 1996, 'Hinduism and Ayurveda: Implications for managing mental health', in D. Bhugra (ed.) *Psychiatry and Religion: Context, Consensus, and Controversies*, London: Routledge.

Biale, D., 1983, 'Eros and enlightenment: Love against marriage in the Eastern European Jewish enlightenment', *Polin*, 1, 50–67.

Birtchnell, J., 1997, 'Attachment in an interpersonal context', *British Journal of Medical Psychology*, 70, 265–280.

Blackmore, S., 1993, *Dying to Live: Near-Death Experiences*, Buffalo, New York: Prometheus.

Bowlby, J., 1969, *Attachment and Loss: Vol 1. Attachment*, New York: Basic Books.

Bowlby, J., 1973, *Attachment and Loss: Vol. 2. Separation: Anxiety and Anger*, New York: Basic Books.

Bowlby, J., 1980, *Attachment and Loss: Vol. 3. Loss*, New York: Basic Books.

Bragan, K., 1977, 'The psychological gains and losses of religious conversion', *British Journal of Medical Psychology*, 50, 177–180.

Brewin, C., 1988, *Cognitive Foundations of Clinical Psychology*, Hillsdale, New Jersey: Lawrence Erlbaum.

Brody, G.H. and Shaffer, D.R., 1982, 'Contributions of parents and peers to children's moral socialisation', *Developmental Review*, 2, 31–75.

Brody, G.H., Stoneman, Z. and Flor, D., 1998, 'Parental religiosity and youth competence', *Developmental Psychology*, 32, 696–707.

Brown, G.A., Spilka, B. and Cassidy, S., 1978, 'The structure of mystical experience and pre- and post-experience lifestyle correlates', Paper presented at the annual conference of the Society for the Scientific Study of Religion, Hartford, Connecticut, October 1978.

Brown, L.B., 1987, *The Psychology of Religious Belief*, London: Academic Press.

Brown, L.B., 1994, *The Human Side of Prayer*, Birmingham, Alabama: Religious Education Press.

Brown, J., in preparation, *Beliefs and Crises*, PhD: University of London.

Brown R., 1965, *Social Psychology*, 1st edtn., New York and London: Macmillan/Free Press.

Buckley, P. and Galanter, M., 1979, 'Mystical experience, spiritual knowledge and a contemporary ecstatic religion', *British Journal of Medical Psychology*, 52, 281–289.

Bufford, R.K., Paloutzian, R.F. and Ellison, C.W., 1991, 'Norms for the Spiritual Well-Being Scale', *Journal of Psychology and Theology*, 19, 56–70.

Cairns, E., 1982, 'Intergroup conflict in Northern Ireland', in H. Tajfel (ed.). *Social Identity and Intergroup Relations*. Cambridge: Cambridge University Press.

Campion, J. and Bhugra, D., 1998, 'Religious and indigenous treatment of mental illness in South India – a descriptive study', *Mental Health, Religion and Culture*, 1, 21–29.

Campion, J. and Bhugra, D., 1997, 'Experiences of healing of psychiatric patients in South India', *Social Psychiatry and Psychiatric Epidemiology*, 32, 215–221.

Capps, D., 1994, 'Religion and child abuse: perfect together', Presidential address of the Society for the Scientific Study of Religion 1991, Pittsburgh, Pennsylvania, *Journal for the Scientific Study of Religion*, 31, 1–14.

Capps, D., 1997, *Men, Religion and Melancholia: James, Otto, Jung and Erikson*, New Haven and London: Yale University Press.

Cinnirella, M. and Loewenthal, K.M., 1999 'Religious influences on beliefs about mental illness in minority groups: a qualitative interview study', *British Journal of Medical Psychology*, in press.

Clark, J., 1979, 'Cults', *Journal of the American Medical Association*, 242, 279–281.

Clarke, P.B., 1988, 'Islam in contemporary Europe', in S. Sutherland, (ed.) *The World's Religions*, 498–519, London: Routledge.

Codol, J.P., 1975, 'On the so-called "superior conformity of the self" behaviour: Twenty experimental investigations', *European Journal of Social Psychology*, 5, 457–501.

Cohen, R.M., Nordahl, T.E, Semple, W.E., Andreason, P. and Pickar, D., 1998, 'Abnormalities in the distributed network of sustained attention predict neuroleptic treatment response in schizophrenia', *Neuropsychopharmacology*, 19, 36–47.

Collins, N.L. and Read, S.J., 1990, 'Adult attachment, working models, and relationship quality in dating couples', *Journal of Personality and Social Psychology*, 58, 644–663.

Colquhoun, F., 1955, *Harringay Story*, London: Hodder & Stoughton.

Cooper, H., 1996, '"The cracked crucible": Judaism and mental health', in D. Bhugra (ed.) *Psychiatry and Religion: Context, Consensus, and Controversies*, London: Routledge.

Cooper-Greene, E.-J., 1998, 'Intrinsic religious orientation and beliefs about sexual morality', BSc Psychology Project, Royal Holloway, University of London.

Cox, J., 1998, 'The psychiatrist as gatekeeper: Reflections on contemporary community psychiatry and the contribution of Paul Tournier', in the Fourth Biennial Conference on Religion and Psychiatry: *Multicultural Psychiatry in a Multifaith Society*, Institute of Psychiatry, London 1998.

Craissati, J., 1990, 'Mental health care in India', *The Psychologist*, 3, 19–22.

Darley, H., 1972, *Slaves and Ivory: A Record of Adventure and Exploration in the Unknown Sudan, and Among the Abyssinian Slave-Raiders*, Northbrook, Illinois: Metro Books. (1st edtn. 1926, London: Witherby).

Day, J., 1993, 'Speaking of belief: Language, performance and narrative in the psychology of religion', *International Journal for the Psychology of Religion*, 3, 213–230.

De Silva, P., 1996, 'Buddhist psychology and implications for treatment', in D. Bhugra (ed.) *Psychiatry and Religion: Context, Consensus, and Controversies*, London: Routledge.

Debo, A., 1970, *A History of the Indians of the United States*, Oklahoma: University of Oklahoma Press. (1995 edn.: London: Random House/Pimlico).

Dein, S., 1996, 'Possession', in K. M. Loewenthal (ed.) *Religious issues in mental health among minority groups: Issues in Britain in the 1990s*, a symposium under the auspices of the Applied Psychology Research Group, Chairman: R.J. West, November 1996, Royal Holloway College, University of London.

Dein, S. and Loewenthal, K.M., 1998, Editorial. *Mental Health, Religion and Culture*, 1, 5–9.

Dickie, J.R., Eshleman, A.K., Merasco, D.M., Shepard, A., Vander Wilt M. and Johnson, M., 1997, 'Parent-child relationships and children's images of God', *Journal for the Scientific Study of Religion*, 36, 25–43.

Dodge, J., Armitage, J. and Kasch, H., 1964, (eds.) *Encyclopaedia Britannica*, London: William Benton.

Donaldson, M., 1987, *Children's Minds*, (originally published 1978), London: Fontana.

Durkheim, E., 1952, *Suicide*, London: Routledge.

El Azayem, G.A. and Hedayat-Diba, Z., 1994, 'The psychological Aspects of Islam: Basic Principles of Islam and their psychological corollary', *International Journal for the Psychology of Religion*, 4, 41–50.

Eliade, M., 1985, *A History of Religious Ideas*, (translated by A. Hiltebeitel and D. Apostolos-Cappadona), London and Chicago: University of Chicago Press.

Elkind, D., 1964, 'Piaget's semi-clinical interview and the study of spontaneous religion', *Journal for the Scientific Study of Religion*, 4, 40–47.

Elkind, D., 1971, 'The development of religious understanding in children and adolescents', in M. Strommen (ed.), *Research on Religious Development: A Comprehensive Handbook. A Project of the Religious Education Association*, New York: Hawthorn Books.

Ellison, C.W., 1983, 'Spiritual well-being: Conceptualization and measurement', *Journal of Psychology and Theology*, 11, 330–340.

Emler, N., Palmer-Canton, E. and St James, A., 1998, 'Politics, moral reasoning and the Defining Issues Test: A reply to Barnett *et al.* (1995)', *British Journal of Social Psychology*, 37, 457–476.

English, H.B. and English A.C., 1958, *A Comprehensive Dictionary of Psychological and Psychoanalytic Terms: A Guide to Usage*, New York, London and Toronto: Longmans Green.

Ensinck, K. and Robertson, B., 1999, Patient and family experiences of psychiatric services and African indigenous healers, *Transcultural Psychiatry*, 36, 23–43.

Erikson, E.H., 1958, *Young Man Luther: A Study in Psychoanalysis and History*, New York: W. W. Norton.

Erikson, E.H., 1963, *Childhood and Society*, New York: Norton.

Ernsberger, D.J. and Manaster, G.L., 1981, 'Moral development, intrinsic/extrinsic religious orientation, and denominational teaching', *Genetic Psychology Monographs*, 104, 23–41.

Esmail, A., 1996, 'Islamic communities and mental health', in D. Bhugra (ed.) *Psychiatry and Religion: Context, Consensus, and Controversies*, London: Routledge.

Esau, T.G., 1998, 'The evangelical Christian in psychotherapy', *American Journal of Psychotherapy*, 52, 28–36.

Evarts, A.B., 1914, 'Dementia Praecox in the coloured race', *Psychoanalytic Review*, 1, 388–403.

Eysenck, H.J. and Eysenck, M.W., 1985, *Personality and Individual Differences*, New York: Plenum.

Eysenck, M.W., 1998, 'Personality and the psychology of religion', *Mental Health, Religion and Culture*, 1, 11–19.

Falbo, T. and Shepperd, J.A., 1986, 'Self-righteousness: cognitive power and religious characteristics', *Journal of Research in Personality*, 20, 145–157.

Fenwick, P., 1987, 'Meditation and the EEG. in M.A. West (ed.) *The Psychology of Meditation*, Oxford: Clarendon Press.

Fenwick, P., 1996, 'The neurophysiology of religious experience', in D. Bhugra (ed.) *Psychiatry and Religion: Context, Consensus, and Controversies*, London: Routledge.

Finn, M. and Gartner, J. (eds.), 1992, *Object Relations Theory and Religion: Clinical Applications*, Westport, Connecticut: Praeger.

Firth, S., 1997, *Dying, Death and Bereavement in a British Hindu Community*, Leuven: Peeters.

Fontana, D., 1980, 'Some standardisation data for the Sandler-Hazari Obsessionality Inventory', *British Journal of Medical Psychology*, 53, 267–275.

Foskett, J., 1996, 'Christianity and psychiatry', in D. Bhugra (ed.) *Psychiatry and Religion: Context, Consensus, and Controversies*, London: Routledge.

Foulds, G.A. and Bedford, A., 1975, 'Hierarchy of classes of personal illness', *Psychological Medicine*, 8, 181–192.

Fowler, J.W., 1981, *Stages of Faith: the Psychology of Human Development and the Quest for Meaning*, San Francisco: Harper and Row.

Fowler, J.W., Nipkow, K.E. and Schweitzer, F. (eds.), 1991, *Stages of Faith and Religious Development: Implications for Church, Education and Society*, New York: Crossroad Publishing.

Francis, L.J., 1992, 'Is psychoticism really a dimension of personality fundamental to religiosity?', *Personality and Individual Differences*, 13, 645–652.

Francis, L.J., 1993a, 'Personality and religion among college students in the UK', *Personality and Individual Differences*, 14, 619–622.

Francis, L.J., 1993b, 'Reliability and validity of a short scale of attitude toward Christianity among adults', *Psychological Reports*, 72, 615–618.

Francis, L.J., Brown, L.B. and Philipchalk, R., 1992, 'The development of an abbreviated form of the Revised Eysenck Personality Questionnaire (EPQR-A): Its use among students in England, Canada, the USA and Australia', *Personality and Individual Differences*, 13, 443–449.

Freud, S., 1907, 'Obsessive acts and religious practices', *Collected Papers*, 1907/1924. London: Hogarth Press.

Freud, S., 1927, *The Future of an Illusion*, London: Hogarth Press.

Freud, S., 1928, *Totem and Taboo: Resemblances between the Psychic Lives of Savages and Neurotics*, New York: Dodd.

Freud, S., 1930 *Civilisation and its Discontents*, London: Hogarth Press.

Freud, S., 1939, *Moses and Monotheism*, London: Hogarth Press and the Institute of Psychoanalysis.

Freud, S., 1958, 'The "uncanny"', in B. Nelson (ed.) *On Creativity and the Unconscious*, A. Strachey (trans.), New York: Harper & Row.

Freud, S., 1963, 'Mourning and melancholia', in P. Rieff (ed.) *General Psychological Theory: Papers on Metapsychology*, J. Riviere (trans.), New York: Collier Books.

Fromm, E., 1950, *Psychoanalysis and Religion*, New Haven: Yale University Press.

Fugate, J.R., 1980, *What the Bible Says About ... Child Training*, Garland, Texas: Aletheia Publishers.

Fulford, K.W.M., 1999, 'From culturally sensitive to culturally competent', in K. Bhui and D. Olajide (eds.), *Mental Health Service Provision for a Multi-Cultural Society*, London: W.B. Saunders.

Furnham, A. and Brown, L.B., 1992, 'Theodicy: A neglected aspect of the psychology of religion', *International Journal for the Psychology of Religion*, 2, 36–46.

Furnham, A. and Procter, E., 1989, 'Belief in a just world: Review and critique of the individual difference literature', *British Journal of Social Psychology*, 28, 365–384.

Galanter, M., Rabkin, R., Rabkin, J. and Deutsch, A., 1979, 'The "Moonies" – a psychological study of conversion and membership in a contemporary religious sect', *American Journal of Psychiatry*, 136, 165–170.

Galanter, M. (ed.), 1989, *Cults and New Religious Movements*, Washington, DC: American Psychiatric Association.

Galton, F., 1883, *Inquiries into Human Faculty and Development*, New York: Macmillan.

Ganzevoort, R.R., 1998a, 'Religious coping reconsidered, Part One: An integrated approach', *Journal of Psychology and Theology*, 26, 270–275.

Ganzevoort, R.R., 1998b 'Religious coping reconsidered, Part Two: A narrative reformulation', *Journal of Psychology and Theology*, 26, 276–286.

Geels, A., 1996, 'A note on the psychology of Dhikr: The Halveti Jerrahi order of dervishes in Istanbul', *International Journal for the Psychology of Religion*, 6, 229–252.

Gergen, K.J., 1993, 'Belief as a relational resource', *International Journal for the Psychology of Religion*, 3, 231–236.

Gilbert, K., 1992, 'Religion as a resource for bereaved parents', *Journal of Religion and Health*, 31, 19–30.

Gilligan, C., 1993, *In a Different Voice: Psychological Theory and Women's Development*, Cambridge, Massachusetts: Harvard University Press.

Glock, C.Y. and Stark, R., 1965, *Religion and Society in Tension*, Chicago: Rand McNally.

Goldman, R., 1964, *Religious Thinking from Childhood to Adolescence*, London: Routledge & Kegan Paul.

Grace, C.R. and Poelstra, P.L. (eds.), 1995, *Journal of Psychology and Theology, Special Issue: An Exploration of Integrative Issues in Undergraduate Psychology Programs*.

Grady, B. and Loewenthal, K.M., 1997, 'Features associated with speaking in tongues (glossolalia)', *British Journal of Medical Psychology*, 70, 185–191.

Greenberg, D., 1997, 'Religious and compulsive rituals: Common features', paper given at the *World Psychiatric Association*, Jerusalem, Israel, November 1997.

Greenberg, D. and Witztum, E., 1991, 'The treatment of obsessive-compulsive disorder in strictly religious patients', in M. T. Pato and J. Zohar (eds.) *Current Treatment of Obsessive Compulsive Disorder*, American Psychiatric Association.

Greenberg, D. and Witztum, E., 1994, 'The influence of cultural factors on obsessive compulsive disorders: Religious symptoms in a religious society', *Israel Journal of Psychiatry and Related Sciences*, 31, 211–220.

Greenberg D., Witztum, E. and Pisante, J., 1987, 'Scrupulosity: Religious attitudes and clinical presentations', *British Journal of Medical Psychology*, 60, 29–37.

Griffith, E.E.H. and Bility, K.M., 1996, 'Psychosocial factors and the genesis of new African-American religious groups', in D. Bhugra (ed.), *Psychiatry and Religion: Context, Consensus, and Controversies*, London: Routledge.

Hardy, A., 1965, *The Living Stream*, London: Collins.

Hardy, A., 1966, *The Divine Flame*, London: Collins.

Hardy, A., 1975, *The Biology of God*, London: Jonathan Cape.

Hardy, A., 1979, *The Spiritual Nature of Man*, Oxford: Clarendon Press.

Harris, T.O., 1997, 'Adult attachment processes and psychotherapy: A commentary on Bartholomew and Birtchnell', *British Journal of Medical Psychology*, 70, 281–290.

Hay, D., 1987, *Exploring Inner Space: Scientists and Religious Experience*, 2nd edn., London: Mowbray.

Hay, D., 1994, '"The Biology of God": What is the current status of Hardy's hypothesis?' *International Journal for the Psychology of Religion*, 4, 1–23.

Hay, D. and Morisy, A., 1978, 'Reports of ecstatic paranormal or religious experience in Great Britain and the United States – A comparison of trends', *Journal for the Scientific Study of Religion*, 17, 255–268.

Hedayat-Diba, Z., 1997, 'The Selfobject functions of the Koran', *International Journal for the Psychology of Religion*, 7, 211–236.

Heirich, M., 1977, 'Change of heart: a test of some widely-held theories about religious conversion', *American Journal of Sociology*, 83, 653–680.

Helminiak, D.A., 1996, 'A scientific spirituality: The interface of Psychology and Theology', *International Journal for the Psychology of Religion*, 6, 1–20.

Hester, M.P., 1998, 'The status of Psychology of Religion: An interview with Raymond F. Paloutzian', *Teaching of Psychology*, 25, 303–306.

Hewstone, M., Islam, M.R. and Judd, C.M., 1993, 'Models of crossed categorization and intergroup relations', *Journal of Personality and Social Psychology*, 64, 779–793.

Hoffman, M.L., 1970, 'Moral development', in P.H. Mussen (ed.), *Carmichael's Manual of Child Psychology*, Vol. 2, New York: Wiley.

Holm, N.G., 1987, 'Sunden's role theory and glossolalia', *Journal for the Scientific Study of Religion*, 26, 383–389.

Hood, R.W., Jr., 1975, 'The construction and preliminary validation of a measure of reported mystical experience', *Journal for the Scientific Study of Religion*, 14, 29–41.

Hood, R.W., Jr., 1992, 'Sin and guilt in faith traditions: Issues for self-esteem', in J. Schumaker (ed.) *Religion and Mental Health*, Oxford: Oxford University Press.

Hunter, J.A., Stringer, M. and Watson, R. P., 1991, 'Intergroup violence and intergroup attributions', *British Journal of Social Psychology*, 30, 261–266.

Husain, S.A., 1998, 'Religion and mental health from the Muslim perspective', in H.G. Koenig (ed.), *Handbook of Religion and Mental Health*, New York: Academic Press.

Huxley, A., 1954, *The Doors of Perception*, New York: Harper.

Idler, E.L., 'Religion, health and nonphysical senses of self', *Social Forces*, 74, 663–704.

Ineichen, B., 1998, 'The influence of religion on the suicide rate: Islam and Hinduism compared', *Mental Health, Religion and Culture*, 1, 31–36.

Ionescu, S., 1998, *Women in the Japanese New Religious Movements in Germany: The Understanding and Construction of the Self*, PhD: Kings College, London University.

Jackson, C., 1996, *Understanding Psychological Testing*, Leicester: British Psychological Society.

Jackson, M.C. and Fulford, K.W.M., 1997, 'Spiritual experience and psychopathology', *Philosophy, Psychiatry and Psychology*, 1, 41–65.

Jacobs, J., 1987, 'Deconversion from religious movements: an analysis of charismatic bonding and spiritual commitment', *Journal for the Scientific Study of Religion*, 26, 294–308.

Jacobson, J., 1997, 'Religion and ethnicity: Dual and alternative sources of identity among young British Pakistanis', *Ethnic and Racial Studies*, 20, 238–256.

Jahangir, F., ur Rehman, H. and Jan, T., 1998, 'Degree of religiosity and vulnerability to suicide attempts/plans among Afghan refugees', *International Journal for the Psychology of Religion*, 8, 265–269.

James, W., 1902, *The Varieties of Religious Experience*, New York: Collier.

Janis, I., 1982, *Groupthink*, 2nd Edtn., Boston, Massachusetts: Houghton Mifflin.

Janoff-Bulman, R., 1979, 'Characterological versus behavioral self-blame: Inquiries into depression and rape', *Journal of Personality and Social Psychology*, 37, 1798–1809.

Johnson, P.E., 1956, *Psychology of Religion*, 2nd Edtn., Nashville, Tennessee: Abingdon.

Jones, E., 1953, *The Life and Work of Sigmund Freud*, vol 1, New York: Basic Books.

Jones, E., 1955, *The Life and Work of Sigmund Freud*, vol 2, New York: Basic Books.

Jones, E., 1957, *The Life and Work of Sigmund Freud*, vol 3, New York: Basic Books.

Jung, C.G., 1958, *Psychology and Religion: East and West*, London: Routledge & Kegan Paul.

Jung, C.G., 1969, *Answer to Job*. R. F. C. Hull (trans.), Princeton: Princeton University Press.

Juthani, N.V., 1998, 'Understanding and treating Hindu patients', in H. G. Koenig (ed.), *Handbook of Religion and Mental Health*, New York: Academic Press.

Kamal, Z. and Loewenthal, K.M., 2002, 'Suicide beliefs and behaviour among young Muslims and Hindus in the UK', *Mental Health, Religion and Culture*, 5, 111–118.

Kelly, G.A., 1955, *The Psychology of Personal Constructs*, New York: Norton.

Kerby, J. and Rae, J., 1998, 'Moral identity in action: Young offenders' reports of encounters with the police', *British Journal of Social Psychology*, 439–456.

Khan, H. (in preparation) *Life-events and depression in Asian Muslim women in Britain*. PhD: London University.

Kirkpatrick L.A., 1992, 'An attachment-theory approach to the psychology of religion', *International Journal for the Psychology of Religion*, 2, 3–28.

Kirkpatrick, L.A., 1997, 'A longitudinal study of changes in religious belief and behaviour as a function of individual differences in adult attachment style', *Journal for the Scientific Study of Religion*, 36, 207–217.

Kirkpatrick, L.A. and Shaver, P.R., 1990, 'Attachment theory and religion: Childhood attachments, religious beliefs and conversion', *Journal for the Scientific Study of Religion*, 29, 315–334.

Klein, M., 1932, *The Psycho-Analysis of Children*, London: Hogarth Press.

Klein, M., 1975, *Envy and Gratitude and Other Works 1946–63*, London: Hogarth Press.

Koenig, H.G., Pargament, K.L. and Nielsen, J., 1998, 'Religious coping and health status in medically ill hospitalized older adults', *Journal of Nervous and Mental Diseases*, 186, 513–521.

Kohlberg, L., 1968, 'The child as a moral philosopher', *Psychology Today*, 2, 25–30.

Kohlberg, L., 1969, 'Stage and sequence: the cognitive-developmental approach to socialization', in D.D. Goslin (ed.) *Handbook of Socialization Theory and Research*, Skokie, Illinois: Rand McNally.

Kose, A., 1996a, *Conversion to Islam: A Study of Native British Converts*, London: Kegan Paul.

Kose, A., 1996b, 'Religious conversion: Is it an adolescent phenomenon? The case of native British converts to Islam' *International Journal for the Psychology of Religion*, 6, 253–262.

Kose, A. and Loewenthal, K.M., 1999, 'Conversion motifs among British converts to Islam', *International Journal for the Psychology of Religion*, in press.

Kroll, J. and Bachrach, B., 1982, 'Visions and psychopathology in the Middle Ages', *Journal of Nervous and Mental Diseases*, 190, 41–49.

Latkin, C.A., 1993, 'Coping after the Fall: The mental health of former members of the Rajneeshpuram commune', *International Journal for the Psychology of Religion*, 3, 97–110.

Lazarus, A.A. and Colman, A.M. (eds.), 1995, *Abnormal Psychology*, London and New York: Longman.

Lederach, N.K. and Lederach, J.P., 1987, 'Religion and psychiatry: Cognitive dissonance in nursing students', *Journal of Psychosocial Nursing and Mental health Services*, 25, 32–36.

Leff, J., 1993, 'Comment on crazy talk: thought disorder or psychiatric arrogance', *British Journal of Medical Psychology*, 66, 77–78.

Lerner, M.J., 1980, *The Belief in a Just World: A Fundamental Delusion*, New York: Plenum.

Lerner, M.J. 1991, 'The belief in a just world and the "Heroic Motive": Searching for "constants" in the psychology of religious ideology, *International Journal for the Psychology of religion*, 1, 27–32.

Levav, I., Kohn, R., Dohrenwend, B.P., Shrout, P.E., Skodol, A.E., Schwartz, S., Link, B.G. and Naveh, G., 1993, 'An epidemiological study of mental disorders in a 10-year cohort of young adults in Israel', *Psychological Medicine*, 23, 691–707.

Levav, I., Kohn, R., Golding, J.M. and Weissman, M.M., 1997, 'Vulnerability of Jews to affective disorders', *American Journal of Psychiatry*, 154, 941–947.

Levin, J.S., 1994, 'Religion and health: Is there an association, is it valid, and is it causal?', *Social Science and Medicine*, 38, 1475–1482.

Levin, J.S. and Chatters, L.M., 1998, 'Research on religion and mental health: An overview of empirical findings and theoretical issues', in H.G. Koenig (ed.) *Handbook of Religion and Mental Health*, New York: Academic Press.

Levitz, I.N., 1992, 'The impact of the marriage imperative on Jewish life', *Journal of Psychology and Judaism*, 16, 109–122.

Lewis, C.A., 1994, 'Religiosity and obsessionality: The relationship between Freud's "religious practices"', *Journal of Psychology*, 189–196.

Lewis, C.A., 1998, 'Cleanliness is next to Godliness: Religiosity and obsessiveness', *Journal of Religion and Health*, 37, 49–61.

Lewis, C.A., 1999a, 'Is the relationship between religion and personality "contaminated" by social desirability as assessed by the Lie Scale?: A methodological reply to Eysenck (1998)', *Mental Health, Religion and Culture*, in press.

Lewis, C.A., 1999b, personal communication.

Lewis, C.A. and Joseph, S., 1994, 'Religiosity: Psychoticism and obsessionality in Northern Irish university students', *Personality and Individual Differences*, 17, 685–687.

Lewis, C.A. and Maltby, J., 1994, 'Religious attitudes and obsessional personality traits among UK adults', *Psychological Reports*, 75, 353–354.

Lewis, I.M., 1971, *Ecstatic Religion*, Baltimore: Penguin.

Linehan, M.M., Goodstein, J.L., Nielsen, S.L. and Chiles, J.A., 1983, 'Reasons for staying alive when you are thinking of killing yourself: The Reasons for Living Inventory', *Journal of Consulting and Clinical Psychology*, 51, 276–286.

Lipsedge, M., 1996, 'Religion and madness in history', in D. Bhugra (ed.) *Psychiatry and Religion: Context, Consensus, and Controversies*, London: Routledge.

Littlewood, R. and Dein, S., 1995, 'The effectiveness of words: Religion and healing among the Lubavitch of Stamford Hill', *Culture, Medicine and Psychiatry*, 19, 330–383.

Littlewood, R. and Lipsedge, M., 1981, 'Acute psychotic reactions in Caribbean-born patients', *Psychological Medicine*, 11, 303–318.

Littlewood, R. and Lipsedge, M., 1989, *Aliens and Alienists: Ethnic Minorities and Psychiatry* 2nd edtn., London: Unwin Hyman.

Littlewood, R. and Lipsedge, M., 1998, 'A religious interest questionnaire for use with psychiatric patients', *Mental Health, Religion and Culture*, 1, 57–63.

Loewenthal, K.M., 1988, 'Religious development and experience in Habad-Hasidic women', *Journal of Psychology and Judaism*, 1988, 12, 5–20.

Loewenthal, K.M., 1995, *Religion and Mental Health*, London: Chapman & Hall.

Loewenthal, K.M., 1996, *An Introduction to Psychological Tests and Scales*, London: UCL Press.

Loewenthal, K.M., 1997, 'Religious beliefs about illness', *International Journal for the Psychology of religion*, 7, 173–178.

Loewenthal, K.M., 1999, 'Religious issues and their psychological aspects', in K. Bhui and D. Olajide (eds.), *Mental Health Service Provision for a Multi-Cultural Society*, London: W. B. Saunders.

Loewenthal, K.M. and Cinnirella, M., 1999a, 'Beliefs about the efficacy of religious, medical and psychotherapeutic interventions for depression and schizophrenia among women from different cultural-religious groups in Great Britain', *Transcultural Psychiatry*, in press.

Loewenthal, K.M. and Cinnirella, M., 1999b, 'Religious issues in ethnic minority mental health with special reference to schizophrenia in Afro-Caribbeans in Britain: A systematic review', in D. Ndegwa and D. Olajide (eds.) *Main Issues in Mental Health and Race*, London: Ashgate.

Loewenthal, K.M., Goldblatt, V., Gorton, T., Lubitsh, G., Bicknell, H., Fellowes, D. and Sowden, A., 1995, 'Gender and depression in Anglo-Jewry', *Psychological Medicine*, 25, 1051–1063.

Loewenthal, K.M., Goldblatt, V., Gorton, T., Lubitsh, G., Bicknell, H., Fellowes, D. and Sowden, A., 1997a, 'The costs and benefits of boundary maintenance: Stress, religion and culture among Jews in Britain', *Social Psychiatry and Psychiatric Epidemiology*, 32, 200–207.

Loewenthal, K.M., Goldblatt, V., Gorton, T., Lubitsh, G., Bicknell, H., Fellowes, D. and Sowden, A., 1997b, 'The social circumstances of anxiety and its symptoms among Anglo-Jews', *Journal of Affective Disorders*, 46, 87–94.

Loewenthal, K.M., Goldblatt, V. and Lubitsh, G., 1998, 'Haredi women, Haredi men, stress and distress', *Israel Journal of Psychiatry and Related Sciences*, 35, 217–224.

Loewenthal, K.M., MacLeod, A.K., Goldblatt, V., Lubitsh, G. and Valentine, J.D., 2000, 'Comfort and Joy? Religion, cognition and mood in individuals under stress', *Cognition and Emotion*, 355–374.

Loewenthal, N., 1990, *Communicating the Infinite: The Emergence of the Habad School*, Chicago and London: University of Chicago Press.

Lofland, J. and Skonovd, N., 1981, 'Conversion motifs', *Journal for the Scientific Study for Religion*, 20, 373–385.

Long, T.R. and Hadden, J.K., 1983, 'Religious conversion and the concept of socialization: Integrating the brainwashing and drift models', *Journal for the Scientific Study of Religion*, 22, 1–14.

Luyten, P., Corveleyn, J. and Fontaine, J.R.J., 1998, 'The relationship between religiosity and mental health: Distinguishing between shame and guilt', *Mental Health, Religion and Culture*, 1, 165–184.

Malony, H.N. and Lovekin, A.A., 1985, *Glossolalia: Behavioural Science Perspectives on Speaking Tongues*, New York: Oxford University Press.

Manne-Lewis, J., 1986, 'Buddhist Psychology: A paradigm for the psychology of enlightenment', in G. Claxton (ed.) *Beyond Therapy: The Impact of Eastern Religions on Psychological Theory and Practice*, London: Wisdom.

Marcia, J.E., 1966, 'Development and validation of ego-identity statuses', *Journal of Personality and Social Psychology*, 3, 119–133.

Maslow, A.H., 1964, *Religions, Values and Peak Experiences*, Columbus: Ohio State University Press.

Masters, R.E.L. and Houston, J., 1973, 'Subjective realities', in B. Schwartz (ed.) *Human Connection and the New Media*, Englewood Cliffs: New Jersey: Prentice Hall.

Mathabane, M., 1994, *African Women: Three Generations*, London: Hamish Hamilton.

Maton, K.I., 1989, 'The stress-buffering role of spiritual support: cross-sectional and prospective investigations', *Journal for the Scientific Study of Religion*, 28, 310–323.

McIntosh, D., 1995, 'Religion-as Schema, with implications for the relations between religion and coping', *International Journal for the Psychology of Religion*, 5, 1–16.

McIntosh D.N., Silver, R.C. and Wortman, C.B., 1993, 'Religion's role in adjusting to a negative life event: coping with the loss of a child', *Journal of Personality and Social Psychology*, 65, 812–821.

Mead, G.H., 1934, *Mind, Self and Society*, Chicago: University of Chicago Press.

Meadow, M.J. and Kahoe, R.D., 1984, *Psychology of Religion: Religion in Individual Lives*, Harper & Row: New York.

Miller, G., Fleming, W. and Brown-Anderson, F., 1998, 'Spiritual Well-Being Scale: Ethnic differences between Caucasian and African-Americans', *Journal of Psychology and Theology*, 26, 358–364.

Moody, R.A., 1975, *Life after Life*, Atlanta, Georgia: Mockingbird Books.

Mordechai, T., 1992, *Playing with Fire*, New York: BP Publishers.

Moscovici, S., 1980, 'Towards a theory of conversion behaviour', in L. Berkowitz (ed.), *Advances in Experimental Social Psychology*, vol. 13, 208–239, New York, Academic Press.

Mytton, J. (in preparation), 'The mental health of people raised in strict fundamentalist sects who have subsequently left: An exploratory study'.

Neeleman, J and Persaud, R., 1995, 'Why do psychiatrists neglect religion?', *British Journal of Medical Psychology*, 68, 169–178.

Noam, R., 1992, *The View from Above*, Lakewood, New Jersey: CIS Publishers.

O'Connor, K.V., 1983, *The Structure of Religion: A Repertory Grid Approach*, PhD: University of New South Wales.

Olson, D., 1989, 'Church friendships: Boon or barrier to church growth?' *Journal for the Scientific Study of Religion*, 28, 432–447

Oser, F. and Gmunder, P., 1991, *Religious Judgement: A Developmental Approach*, trans. N.F. Hahn, Birmingham, Alabama: Religious Education Press, 1991.

Osgood, C.E., Suci, G.J. and Tannenbaum, P.H., 1957, *The Measurement of Meaning*, University of Illinois Press.

Otto, R., 1917, *The Idea of the Holy: An Inquiry into the Non-Rational Factor in the Idea of the Divine and its Relation to the Rational*, Oxford: Oxford University Press.

Pahnke, W.N., 1966, 'Drugs and Mysticism', *International Journal of Parapsychology*, 52, 295–324.

Paloutzian, R.F., 1983, *Invitation to the Psychology of Religion*, Glenview, Illinois: Scott Foresman.

Paloutzian, R.F., 1996, *Invitation to the Psychology of Religion*, 2nd Edtn., Massachusetts: Allyn & Bacon.

Paloutzian, R.F. and Ellison, C.W., 1982, 'Loneliness, spiritual well-being and quality of life', in L.A. Peplau and D.A. Perlman (eds.) *Loneliness: A Sourcebook of Current Theory, Research and Therapy*, New York: Wiley Interscience.

Paloutzian, R.F., Richardson, J.T. and Rambo, L.R., 1999, 'Religious conversion and personality change', *Journal of Personality*, in press.

Pargament, K.I. and Brant, C.R., 1998, 'Religion and coping', in H.G. Koenig (ed.) *Handbook of Religion and Mental Health*, New York: Academic Press.

Pargament, K.I., Ensing, D.S., Falgout, K., Olsen, H., Reilly, B., Van Haitsma, K. and Warren, R., 1990, 'God help me: (I): Religious coping efforts as predictors of outcomes to significant negative life events', *American Journal of Community Psychology*, 18, 793–834.

Pargament, K.I. and Hahn, J., 1986, 'God and the just world: Causal and coping attributions to God in health situations', *Journal for the Scientific Study of Religion*, 25, 193–207.

Pargament, K.I., Kennel, J., Hathaway, W., Groevengoed, N., Newman, J. and Jones, W., 1988, 'Religion and the problem-solving process: Three styles of coping', *Journal for the Scientific Study of Religion*, 27, 90–104.

Parker, G.B. and Brown, L.B., 1982, 'Coping behaviours that mediate between life-events and depression', *Archives of General Psychiatry*, 39, 1386–1391.

Parker, W.R. and St. Johns, W.E., 1957, *Prayer Can Change Your Life: Experiments and Techniques in Prayer Therapy*, Carmel, New York: Guideposts Associates.

Penfield, W. and Perot, P., 1963, 'The brain's record of auditory and visual experience', *Brain*, 86, 595–696.

Pettigrew, T., 1979, 'The ultimate attribution error. Extending Allport's cognitive analysis of prejudice', *Personality and Social Psychology Bulletin*, 5, 461–476.

Perez Y Mena, A.I., 1998, 'Cuban Santeria, Haitian Vodun, Puerto Rican Spiritualism: A multicultural enquiry into spiritualism', *Journal for the Scientific Study of Religion*, 37, 15–27.

Peters, E., Day, S., McKenna, J. and Orbach, G., 1999, 'Delusional ideas in religious and psychotic populations', *British Journal of Clinical Psychology*, 38, 83–96.

Pfeifer, S., 1994, 'Belief in demons and exorcism in psychiatric patients in Switzerland', *British Journal of Medical Psychology*, 67, 247–258.

Piaget, J., 1932, *The Moral Judgement of the Child*, New York: Free Press (1965).

Piaget, J., 1967, *Six Psychological Studies*, New York: Random House, Vintage Books.

Pope, L., 1942, *Millhands and Preachers*, New Haven, Connecticut: Yale University Press.

Poston, L.A., 1988, *Islamic "Da'wah" in North America, and the dynamics of conversion*, Ann Arbor: Michigan University Microfilms.

Potter, J. and Wetherell, M., 1987, *Discourse and Social Psychology: Beyond Attitudes and Behaviour*, London: Sage.

Power, M., Champion, L. and Aris, L., 1988, 'The development of a measure of social support: The Significant Others Scale (SOS)', *British Journal of Clinical Psychology*, 27, 349–358.

Prudo, R., Harris, T.O. and Brown, G., 1984, 'Psychiatric disorder in an urban and a rural population. 3: Social integration and the morphology of affective disorder', *Psychological Medicine*, 14, 327–345.

Reich, K.H., 1997, 'Do we need a theory for the religious development of women?' *International Journal for the Psychology of Religion*, 7, 67–86.

Rest, J.R., 1979, *Development in judging moral issues*, Minneapolis: University of Minnesota Press.

Rest, J.R., 1983, 'Morality', in J. Flavell and E. Markham (eds.), *Manual of Child Psychology. Volume 3: Cognitive Development*, P. Mussen, general editor.

Richardson, J.T., 1985, 'Psychological and psychiatric studies of new religions', in L.B.Brown (ed.) *Advances in the Psychology of Religion*, Oxford: Pergamon Press.

Rizzuto, A.M., 1974, 'Object relations and the formation of the image of God', *British Journal of Medical Psychology*, 47, 83–89.

Rizzuto, A.M., 1979, *The Birth of the Living God*, Chicago: University of Chicago Press.

Rizzuto, A.M., 1992, 'Afterword', in M. Finn and J. Gartner (eds.) *Object Relations Theory and Religion: Clinical Applications*, (1992) Westport, Connecticut: Praeger.

Rubin, Z. and Peplau, L.A., 1973, 'Belief in a just world and reactions to another's lot: A study of participants in the national draft lottery', *Journal of Social Issues*, 29, 73–93.

Rubin, Z. and Peplau, L.A., 1975, 'Who believes in a just world?', *Journal of Social Issues*, 31, 65–90.

Samarin, W.J., 1972, *Tongues of Men and Angels: The Religious Language of Pentecostalism*, New York: Macmillan.

Schwieso J.J., 1996, '"Religious fanaticism" and wrongful confinement in Victorian England: The affair of Louisa Nottidge', *The Social History of Medicine*, 9, 158–74.

Scobie, G.W., 1975, *Psychology of Religion*, New York: Wiley.

Scotton, B.W., 1998, 'Treating Buddhist patients', in H. G. Koenig (ed.) *Handbook of Religion and Mental Health*, New York: Academic Press.

Sensky, T. and Fenwick, P., 1982, 'Religiosity, mystical experience and epilepsy', in C. Rose (ed.) *Progress in Epilepsy*, London: Pitman.

Shams, M. and Jackson, P.R., 1993, 'Religiosity as a predictor of well-being and moderator of the psychological impact of unemployment', *British Journal of Medical Psychology*, 66, 341–352.

Shapiro, D.H. and Walsh, R.N. (eds.), 1984, *Meditation: Classic and Contemporary Perspectives*, New York: Aldine.

Shapiro, D.H., 1982, 'Overview: Clinical and physiological comparison of meditation with other self-control strategies', *American Journal of Psychiatry*, 139, 167–174.

Sharma, U., 1971, *Rampal and his Family: The Story of an Immigrant*, London: Collins.

Shaver, P., Lenauer, M. and Sadd, S., 1980, 'Religiousness, conversion and subjective well-being: the "healthy-minded" religion of modern American women', *American Journal of Psychiatry*, 137, 1563–1568.

Shneur Zalman of Liadi, 1973, *Likkutei Amarim – Tanya*, (bilingual ed.; N. Mindel, N. Mandel, Z. Posner and J.I. Shochet, trans.) London: Kehot (original work published in 1796).

Siegman, A.W., 1963, 'A cross-cultural investigation of the relationship between introversion, social attitudes and social behaviour', *British Journal of Social and Clinical Psychology*, 2, 196–208.

Smith, W.C., 1963, *The Meaning and End of Religion: A New Approach to the Religious Traditions of Mankind*, New York: Macmillan.

Smith, W.C., 1979, *Faith and Belief*, Princeton, New Jersey: Princeton University Press.

Snyder, J.G. and Osgood, C.E., 1969, *Semantic Differential Technique*, Chicago: Aldine.

Solomon, V., 1965, *A Handbook on Conversions*, Stravon.

Spero, M.H., 1992, *Religious Objects as Psychological Structures: a Critical Integration of Object Relations Theory, Psychotherapy and Judaism*, Chicago and London: University of Chicago Press.

Spero, M.H., 1987, 'Identity and individuality in the nouveau-religious patient: theoretical and clinical aspects', *Psychiatry*, 50, 55–71.

Spilka, B., Comp, G. and Goldsmith, W.M., 1981, 'Faith and behaviour: Religion in introductory texts of the 1950s and 1970s', *Teaching of Psychology*, 8, 159–160.

Stace, W.T., 1960, *Mysticism and Philosophy*, Philadelphia: Lippincott.

Stanley, G.S., 1964, 'Personality and attitude correlates of religious conversion', *Journal for the Scientific Study of Religion*, 4, 60–63.

Staples C.L. and Mauss, A.L., 1987, 'Conversion or commitment? A reassessment of the Snow and Machalek approach to the study of conversion', *Journal for the Scientific Study of Religion*, 26, 133–147.

Stark, R. and Bainbridge, W.S., 1985, *The Future of Religion*, Berkeley: University of California Press.

Steley, J., 1996, *Parental Discipline and Religious Commitment as Recalled by Adult Children*, unpublished M. Phil. thesis: University of London.

Stouffer, S.A. *et al.*, 1949, *The American Soldier Vol 2: Combat and its Aftermath*, Princeton: Princeton University Press.

Sunden, H., 1959, *Die Religion und die Rollen: Eine psychologische Untersuchung der Fromigkeit*, Berlin: Alfred Topelmann, 1966 (original Swedish edition, 1959).

Tajfel, H., 1970, 'Experiments in intergroup discrimination', *Scientific American*, 223, 96–102.

Tajfel, H., 1978, *Differentiation Between Groups*, Cambridge: Cambridge University Press.

Tajfel, H. and Turner, J., 1986, 'The Social Identity Theory of intergroup behaviour', in S. Worchel and W.G. Austin (eds.) *Psychology of Intergroup Relations*, Chicago: Nelson.

Tangney, J.P., 1995, 'Shame and guilt in interpersonal relationships', in J.P. Tangney and K.W. Fischer (eds.), *Self-conscious Emotions: The Psychology of Shame, Guilt, Embarassment and Pride*, New York: The Guilford Press.

Tangney, J.P., Burggraf, S.A. and Wagner, P.E., 1995, 'Shame-proneness, guilt-proneness, and psychological symptoms. in J.P. Tangney and K.W. Fischer (eds), *Self-conscious Emotions: The Psychology of Shame, Guilt, Embarassment and Pride*, New York: The Guilford Press.

Tauber, Y., 1994, *Once upon a Chassid*, New York: Kehot.

Thun, T., 1959, *Die Religion des Kindes*, 2nd Edtn. Stuttgart: Ernest Klett, 1964.

Turner, J.C., 1987, *Rediscovering the Social Group: A Self-categorization Theory*, Oxford: Basil Blackwell.

Ullman, C., 1982, 'Cognitive and emotional antecedents of religious conversion', *Journal of Personality and Social Psychology*, 43, 183–192.

Valentine, E.R., 1989, 'A cognitive psychological analysis of meditation techniques and mystical experiences', *Ethical Record*, April 1989, 9–20.

Valentine, E.R. and Sweet, P., 1999, 'Meditation and attention: A comparison of the effects of concentrative and mindfulness meditation on attention', *Mental Health, Religion and Culture*, 2, 59–70.

Van Avermaet, E., 1996, 'Social influence in small groups', in M. Hewstone, W. Stroebe and G.M. Stephenson (eds.), *Introduction to Social Psychology*, Oxford: Blackwell.

Vergote, A. and Tamayo, A., 1980, *The Parental Figures and the Representation of God*, The Hague: Mouton.

Watson, P.J., Morris, R.J., Foster, J.E. and Hood, R.W., Jr., 1986, 'Religiosity and social desirability', *Journal for the Scientific Study of Religion*, 25, 215–232.

Watson, P.J., Morris, R.J. and Hood, R.W., Jr., 1988a 'Sin and self-functioning: Part 1: Grace, guilt and self-consciousness', *Journal of Psychology and Theology*, 16, 254–269.

Watson, P.J., Morris, R.J. and Hood, R.W., Jr., 1988b, 'Sin and self-functioning: Part 2: Grace, guilt and psychological adjustment', *Journal of Psychology and Theology*, 16, 270–281.

Watson, P.J., Morris, R.J. and Hood, R.W., Jr., 1988c, 'Sin and self-functioning: Part 3: The psychology and ideology of irrational beliefs', *Journal of Psychology and Theology*, 16, 348–361.

Watson, P.J., Morris, R.J., Hood, R.W., Jr., Milliron, J.T. and Stutz, N. L., 1998, 'Religious orientation, identity, and the quest for meaning in ethics within an ideological surround', *International Journal for the Psychology of Religion*, 8, 149–164.

Watts, F. and Williams, M., 1988, *The Psychology of Religious Knowing*, New York: Cambridge University Press.

Wearing, A.J. and Brown, L.B., 1972, 'The dimensionality of religion', *British Journal of Social and Clinical Psychology*, 11, 143–148.

Weissler, C., 1998, *Voices of the Matriarchs: Listening to the Prayers of Early Modern Jewish Women*, Boston, Massachusetts: Beacon Press.

Wilson, B.R., 1970, *Religious Sects*, London: Weidenfeld and Nicholson.

Winnicott, D., 1958, *Collected Papers: Through Paediatrics to Psycho-Analysis*, London: Tavistock.

Witztum, E., Buchbinder, J.T. and Van Der Hart, O., 1990a, 'Summoning a punishing angel: Treating a depressed patient with dissociative features', *Bulletin of the Menninger Clinic*, 54, 524–537.

Witztum, E., Dasberg, H. and Greenberg, D., 1990b, 'Mental illness and religious change', *British Journal of Medical Psychology*, 63, 33–42.

Worthington, E.L., Kurusu, T.A., McCullough, M.E. and Sandage, S.J., 1996, 'Empirical research on religion and psychotherapeutic processes and outcomes: A 10-year review and research prospectus', *Psychological Review*, 119, 448–487.

Wulff, D.M., 1997, *Psychology of Religion: Classic and Contemporary*, 2nd Edtn., New York: Wiley.

Youngman, R., Minuchin-Itzigsohn, S. and Barasch, M., 1999, 'Manifestations of emotional distress among Ethiopian immigrants in Israel: Patient and clinician perspectives', *Transcultural Psychiatry*, 36, 45–63.

Zinnbauer, B.J., Pargament, K.I., Cole, B., Rye, M.S., Butter, E.M., Belavich, T.G., Hipp, K.M., Scott, A.B. and Kadar, J.L., 1997, 'Religion and spirituality: Unfuzzying the fuzzy', *Journal for the Scientific Study of Religion*, 36, 549–564.

INDEX